ANOINTED *to be*
GOD'S SERVANTS

ANOINTED *to be* GOD'S SERVANTS

HOW GOD BLESSES THOSE
WHO SERVE TOGETHER

HENRY BLACKABY
and
THOMAS BLACKABY

OLIVER
NELSON

™

THOMAS NELSON PUBLISHERS®
Nashville

A Division of Thomas Nelson, Inc.
www.ThomasNelson.com

Published in Nashville, Tennessee, by Thomas Nelson, Inc.

All Scripture quotations, unless otherwise indicated, are taken from the New King James Version®. Copyright © 1982 by Thomas Nelson, Inc. Used by permission. All rights reserved.

Scripture quotations marked CEV are taken from the Contemporary English Version. © 1995 American Bible Society. Used by permission.

Scripture quotations noted ASV are from the Holy Bible, Authorized Standard Version.

Scripture quotations marked HCSB are taken from the Holman Christian Standard Bible, © 2004, Broadman & Holdman Publishers.

Scripture quotations marked ISV are from the International Standard Version © 1998 Davidson Press.

Scripture quotations marked KJV are from the Holy Bible, King James Version.

Scripture quotations marked MKJV are taken from the Modern King James Version, © 1990, Sovereign Grace Publishers.

Scripture quotations noted NIV are taken from the HOLY BIBLE, NEW INTERNATIONAL VERSION®. Copyright © 1973, 1978, 1984 by International Bible Society. Used by permission of Zondervan Bible Publishing House. All rights reserved.

The "NIV" and "New International Version" trademarks are registered in the United States Patent and Trademark Office by International Bible Society. Use of either trademark requires the permission of International Bible Society.

Nelson Books titles may be purchased in bulk for educational, business, fund-raising, or sales promotional use. For information, please e-mail SpecialMarkets@ThomasNelson.com.

Published in association with the literary agency of Wolgemuth & Associates, Inc.

Library of Congress Cataloging-in-Publication Data

Blackaby, Henry T., 1935–
    Anointed to be God's servants : how God blesses those who serve together / Henry Blackaby and Thomas Blackaby.
      p. cm.
    Includes bibliographical references.
    ISBN 0-7852-6205-9 (hardcover)
    1. Fellowship—Religious aspects—Christianity. 2. Paul, the Apostle, Saint—Friends and associates. I. Blackaby, Tom, 1962– II. Title.
    BV4517.5.B56 2005
    253'.2—dc22   2005003503

Printed in the United States of America

05 06 07 08 09 QW 5 4 3 2 1

*To our sons Richard, Thomas, Melvin, and Norman. To our
daughter, Carrie. And to each of their spouses. They have all been
unique and special encouragements to Marilynn and me as we seek
to faithfully serve our Lord together.*
—HENRY T. BLACKABY

*To my wife, Kim, God's lifelong companion to me; to my children,
Erin, Matthew, and Conor; and to the many people who have
walked faithfully with me in ministry. To God be the glory.*
—TOM BLACKABY

Contents

CONTENTS

"Whoever accepts anyone I send accepts me."
—*John 13:20* (NIV)

INTRODUCTION

The Most Difficult Instrument in the Orchestra

LEONARD BERNSTEIN, the American composer, conductor, concert pianist, author, and educator, is quoted as saying, "The hardest instrument in the orchestra to play is second fiddle." This is presumably so because the individual must work just as hard as the first violinist, yet be content with a seemingly subordinate role in the orchestra.

To God, there are no "second fiddlers." Each person has a valuable role to play, and none is more or less important than another. First Corinthians 12 reminds us that as Christ's body, each of us functions both uniquely and interdependently. Some will be chosen to take the lead, while others will be given the tasks of encouragers and companions. None are meant to function independently from the body or in opposition within the body, as all are equally important and dependent.

Scripture and history are full of examples of God's design for leaders and companions in His kingdom; even a cursory glance at the life of Paul reveals an abundance of support for this divine strategy. Many people start their Christian lives with the idea of being like Paul: strong, adventurous, and an outstanding leader in God's kingdom. And there are indeed many notable Christians who have made a tremendous impact on hundreds and thousands of lives over the years. But it appears that God assigns the vast majority of us more of a supportive role, working alongside other more prominent figures in God's kingdom, that is, ministering as companions.

The word *companion* comes from the Greek σύζυγος (*syzugos*), which can essentially be translated "yokefellow; people harnessed together, complementing one another, and pulling with a common purpose and goal." Companionship is one of the primary strategies God uses in His kingdom to accomplish His purposes in and through His people. He desires and intends for believers to receive the companions He puts around them and, at the same time, serve as companions to others.

Even Jesus, the ultimate leader, was assigned by God to have close companions in ministry. Twelve people spent three years learning from and walking with Jesus. Of these twelve, three had a more intimate fellowship and friendship with Christ. On three separate occasions, Jesus asked these special friends to accompany Him. Throughout Christ's ministry, He was also an essential companion to His disciples. After His resurrection, He went to be with the Father but promised (Matt. 28:20) to always be with them.

It is instructive to note that the Father would send the Holy Spirit to be their counselor and companion throughout their lives. "I will ask the Father, and he will give you another Counselor to be with you . . . I will not leave you as orphans" (John 14:16–18 NIV). The word *counselor*, or *paracletos*, means someone who is called alongside as a helper or advocate. The Holy Spirit, our *paracletos*, sets the standard and example for those in God's kingdom to become companions to one another.

As you will see in the coming chapters, serving as a companion is not an easy role, often requiring much stamina and sacrifice. A true companion is someone who dedicates his or her life to helping other individuals follow God's will for their lives. He or she is there to affirm, to encourage, to pray, and to support, often at great personal cost. Paul spoke of Aquila and Priscilla as his "fellow workers in Christ Jesus" who "risked their lives" for him (Rom. 16:3–4), and called Epaphroditus his "fellow worker and fellow soldier," saying of him, "he almost died for the work of Christ, risking his life" (Phil. 2:25, 30).

A companion may also be one who prevents a person from taking self-destructive avenues or compromising positions at difficult times in his or her ministry. George Mueller (1805–1898), a man of great faith and founder of dozens of orphanages caring for hundreds of children, had such a friendship with J. Hudson Taylor (1832–1905), missionary to China.

At one particularly discouraging point in Taylor's ministry, Mueller was there as an encourager. Taylor had been robbed by ruffians of his clothing and equipment; his supplies had burned in a tragic fire; he was destitute, with no promise of any further support; and he was a physical and emotional wreck. Spiraling into depression, he received a letter from Mueller, who encouraged him to live by faith and to continue the fight. Not only did Mueller cheer Taylor with words, but he also personally sent ten thousand dollars annually toward his support. So in June he resigned from the Chinese Evangelization Society at age twenty-five and formed the China Inland Mission to continue the missionary work in China. China Inland Mission established 20 mission stations, brought 849 missionaries to the field (968 by 1911), trained some 700 Chinese workers, raised $4 million by faith (following Mueller's example), and developed a witnessing Chinese church of 125,000 by the time Taylor left the mission field.

A companion may be a brother or sister, as in the case of the evangelists John (1703–1791) and Charles (1707–1788) Wesley, or a good friend, such as George Whitefield (1714–1770) was to John Wesley. The Wesley brothers knew each other well and worked together with a common heart and passion to train others, to boldly preach the Word, and to worship the God they served. But it was Whitefield who invited young John Wesley to preach alongside him when he had been turned out by his church and denomination, helping John on his way to decades-long ministry as a traveling evangelist.

YOU HAVE A VITAL ROLE

Each person plays a vital role in God's kingdom, from the least noticed to the most prominent individual, and each role is just as important as all the others. The key is not how noticed you are or how "effective" you are; it is how *obedient* you are to your Lord and Master. Jesus said, "You are My friends if you do whatever I command you" (John 15:14). Conversely, He said, "Why do you call Me 'Lord, Lord,' and not do the things which I say?" (Luke 6:46). We must be ever mindful of the fact that we are the servants, the ambassadors of a mighty King. He determines our usefulness to His purposes according to how He has gifted and equipped us for ministry. Our primary concern ought to be how well we are serving the Master where He has placed us. It is not what we do *for* God that will count in the end, but what we let God do *through* us and *with* us that will last.

> **The key is not how noticed you are or how "effective" you are; it is how *obedient* you are to your Lord and Master.**

The purpose of this book is to help you understand the incalculable importance companions played in the life of Paul and in the kingdom of God. It is written for the vast majority of Christians who work hard behind the scenes, get little recognition, and are shown infrequent appreciation for the exceedingly important work they do in God's kingdom.

In our own experiences over the years, we have found that some of the greatest gifts of God are the companions He has given us in ministry. The greater the assignment, the more significant these companions became. At each stage in our lives, God has brought a companion to walk with us and encourage us to follow after God and to be obedient to His will for us. We firmly believe that God has deliberately designed His people to be interdependent upon one another in His kingdom. Whatever God has done through our lives has been the result of the combined efforts of many people working together. In some cases whole churches have taken on the role of companion, and we have been able to rejoice together as we watched God work through our lives together.

God has deliberately designed His people to be interdependent upon one another in His kingdom.

We, God's people, must recapture the full recognition of the significant need for God-appointed companions in ministry if we are to achieve the level of impact He intends us to have. All spiritual leaders, particularly those on the mission field, must have companions to undergird their lives and ministries.

I often rejoice at the remembrance of the many companions God has sent us over the years to assist us as we planted churches in Canada. Some, such as Len Koster and Jack Connor, worked alongside us in the daily demands of church planting. Others, like Robert Cannon, came to work with students, to call out the called, those who would pastor the newly planted churches. Barbara Burket, John Cunningham, and Bill Bye came from other cities to teach theology and religious education to the pastors raised up from the student ministry. Bill and Maxine Shadle came up from Texas—every summer for fourteen years—to encourage us, to build churches, to evangelize, and to perform choir music. Others sent funding to support pastor salaries and church property purchases. Individuals and churches who contributed became unique companions as God moved in their hearts to share what He had given them to bless others. Scores of others prayed diligently, and as one, we saw the hand of God at work, doing the incredible through ordinary people working together.

This book is a tribute to hundreds of God's choicest servants who have walked with us as companions over the years, and to those who daily and diligently walk as faithful companions to God's people, wherever He has placed them. Though it will be written from my perspective, it is a thoroughly coauthored work, incorporating anecdotes and insights from both my son Tom's ministry and my own. As Paul was meticulous in naming people who were important to him and to the cause of Christ, we also want to share with you a representative sample of those whom we have greatly appreciated throughout our ministries. Our prayer is that you will come to a new understanding and appreciation for God's strategy of companionship in His kingdom, for *every* believer!

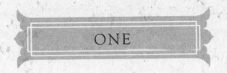

ONE

Paul's Need for Companions

Paul's life was a guided life, not a driven life. As such, God not only directed where he should go, but also with whom he should go. He was a single man, whose God-given task was absolutely impossible to accomplish alone.

If you take a cursory glance at the New Testament church-planting experience, you can see that Paul shines as the dominant figure. But though Paul played a central role, God involved dozens of other men and women, adding their unique perspectives and abilities to the effort. With each new companion in ministry, Paul's life was being shaped according to God's plan. The many dimensions of companionship seen in the life of Paul are very informative and equally eye-opening to those in ministry today. In fact, his entire life and ministry reveal how God purposed for him to have companions and assistants in ministry. Companionship in ministry is not only descriptive of Paul's life, but prescriptive for every Christian in the kingdom of God.

PAUL'S CONVERSION

As the Scriptures reveal the nature and purposes of God, we must not overlook the way God chose for Paul to be converted. As far as God is concerned, His call to salvation is a call to be on a mission with Him. When God "chose us . . . before the creation of the world" and "predestined us to be adopted as his sons through Jesus Christ" (Eph. 1:4–5 NIV) we became "God's workmanship, created in Christ Jesus to do good works, which God prepared in advance for us to do" (2:10 NIV). We can see this documented through the life of Paul.

As far as God is concerned, His call to salvation is a call to be on a mission with Him.

The apostle Paul had a sordid past. A self-righteous tormentor and persecutor of Christians, he even participated in their imprisonment and martyrdom.

One fateful day, Saul of Tarsus (as he was then known) and his companions, with orders from the high priest in Jerusalem, were on their way to arrest followers of Christ in Damascus. But on the way, Saul was thrown to the ground by a blinding light and a thundering voice out of heaven. It was Christ Himself, intersecting Saul's life, and redirecting his path. Saul of Tarsus would become the apostle Paul, a "chosen vessel" (Acts 9:15) to fulfill *Christ's* purposes.

As Saul wallowed on the ground, disabled and blinded by the heavenly light, "the Lord said to him, 'Arise and go into the city, and you will be told what you must do'" (v. 6). Sightless, he had to be taken by the hand and led into the city, where he would meet the men who would welcome him into the kingdom of God, and groom him for his destiny.

Paul's conversion established a pattern for his dependency on others that he would follow for the rest of his life. Had Saul of Tarsus not been with companions during his encounter with Christ, he may have been lost forever, wandering blind in the wilderness. But it was God's deliberate intention that he be *led by the hand* in complete, blind dependence on others.

God made Paul wait three days before being told what to do (Acts 9:9).

He had three long, dark days to process what his life had been. Nothing makes one more dependent on others than total blindness. He felt paralyzed. He was in his darkest hour.

This hardened, bigoted, determined enemy of Christ was led helplessly to the home of Judas on the street called Straight in Damascus (v. 11). There he waited for God's servant, Ananias, who would be used by God to open his eyes both physically and spiritually. The very one he had likely come to imprison was now setting him free from blindness. How humiliating . . . and illuminating!

Jesus once said that the measure with which we measure will be measured back to us (Luke 6:38). God told Ananias, "I will show [Paul] how much he must suffer for my name" (Acts 9:16 NIV). When we follow Paul's life and ministry, we see that no one else had such a great list of sufferings in the service of Christ. As Paul had been the cause of the suffering of God's people, so now he would participate in the sufferings of the churches. Of all the times when interdependence is required, the times we face suffering are at the top of the list. God was true to the prophecy for His call on Paul's life.

> **Of all the times when interdependence is required, the times we face suffering are at the top of the list.**

PAUL'S BEGINNINGS

From the beginning of his Christian life, we find Paul immersed in dependence upon other believers in the early Damascus church, and later in Jerusalem and Antioch. The incredible irony should not be missed: Saul went to Damascus to arrest and imprison disciples, yet God forced him to *be dependent* upon the very ones he had gone to arrest! Ananias, likely a leader among the believers in Damascus, was also going to appreciate more of God's grace and mercy upon a lost soul. True, Paul was going to pay a great price for his crimes, but now it would be as a fellow believer rather than an enemy: the first words out of Ananias's mouth were *"Brother Saul"* (Acts 9:17). There was so much more that Ananias could have said, probably much more that he wanted to say. But as a true servant, he said simply, "The Lord sent me to return your sight."

Here God taught Paul the true nature of His people. What Paul had learned in school and had seen demonstrated by the religious leaders of his day was not what God intended for His people. Love, compassion, and interdependence would replace hatred, bigotry, and self-reliance in Paul's life, and he would become one of the greatest encouragers to God's people that the world would ever see. The same one who had earlier sat at the feet of the great Gamaliel, a respected Pharisee and celebrated doctor of the Law, would soon be seated with simple fishermen, hearing the wonderful stories of the Christ they had followed as disciples. It was Barnabas, a church leader in Jerusalem, who would genuinely see Paul as a brother, full of potential, while others remained suspicious of him (vv. 26–27). Later, Barnabas, whose name means "son of encouragement," left Jerusalem to search for Paul in Tarsus (Acts 11). When Barnabas found him, he brought Paul to Antioch, where they ministered together for more than a year, strengthening this new international church.

It was this same church in Antioch that would later commission the two as missionaries, laying their hands on them and blessing them as they were sent. Paul and Barnabas took with them the nephew of Barnabas, John Mark, who was destined to play a significant role in Paul's later years. From the beginning of Paul's ministry, God brought other faithful men like Barnabas along with Paul to help sharpen and focus his vision for ministry and his skills in presenting the message.

I believe it is enlightening to us that we have no record of the apostle Paul ever setting out on a missionary journey without a companion at his side. The only time Paul traveled on his own was when he debated with the philosophers in Athens. Only a few in Athens were believers, and there is no evidence that a church was established from this lone mission excursion. Yet even here, Paul instructed his traveling companions, Silas and Timothy, to join him as quickly as possible. It is no wonder that many church-planting strategies today involve sending out teams of people.

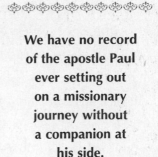

We have no record of the apostle Paul ever setting out on a missionary journey without a companion at his side.

PAUL LEARNED EARLY THE IMPORTANCE OF COMPANIONSHIP

Companionship was not only invaluable to individuals, but also to entire churches. Clearly, Paul had individual traveling companions, who served many purposes in his life and upon whom he became very dependent throughout his ministry. But Paul also learned the importance of developing a network of interdependence between himself and the churches to whom he ministered. They would become his "lifeblood" for encouragement and support during both the good times and the times of persecution and suffering. He said in his letter to the Thessalonians, "Brothers, pray for us" (1 Thess. 5:25). This was an invitation to a whole church to join him in his missionary efforts, and in return Paul demonstrates prayer *for them*: "Therefore we also pray always for you that our God would count you worthy of the calling and fulfill all the good pleasure of His goodness and the work of faith with power" (2 Thess. 1:11).

I can't help but think of the great missionary William Carey, who in 1793 said, "I will venture to go down, but remember that you must hold the ropes." Paul said it this way in Ephesians 6:18: "Stay alert and keep praying for God's people" (CEV). It is imperative that churches be companions to those who are sent. The church in Antioch was like the sponsoring church—more than simply sending out Paul and Barnabas, they were involved through giving, praying, and supporting in any way they were able.

The church in Ephesus also felt responsible to support and encourage Paul. The idea of mutual interdependence spread throughout the churches, with Paul as one of the uniting factors. He was instrumental in encouraging the churches in Asia Minor to take on the responsibility of being supporters and encouragers to the church in Jerusalem when it was in need. It was a testimony to their love for Christ that these Gentile churches aided the Jewish church, the original church, in Jerusalem.

NOT JUST FOR THE CLERGY

Supporting and encouraging God's servants must not be left to only professional ministers. Parents and families, too, can make mission trips to help missionaries and be involved in their support in hundreds of different ways, from sending money or supplies to spending weeks or months assisting in the work. Taking children with you on missions will change their lives forever! There are ways of partnering with missionaries and ministries that can be a tremendous encouragement to God's people. A single church or a group of churches can undergird ministries with money, resources, supplies, and prayers. Romans 16:16 (NIV) says, "All the churches of Christ send their greetings."

> **Taking children with you on missions will change their lives forever!**

As a married couple, you might choose to come alongside other couples in ministry as companions, mentors, and encouragers, and walk with them as God uses them in His kingdom. At the very least, we all ought to find others to invest our lives in so that together we can make tremendous contributions to God's work.

NEEDY TIMES IN PAUL'S LIFE

Because Paul was new to ministry and unproven among the apostles, he needed someone to corroborate his reports to the churches in Antioch and Jerusalem (Acts 14:27, 15:12). God provided Barnabas, a dignified and commanding prophet and teacher, well-respected among these congregations. Paul had seen God's tremendous work among Gentile believers, but some men from Jerusalem, called Judaizers, were insisting the Gentiles be subject to Jewish law before they could be considered Christians. This went against everything Paul had learned from Christ, who had taught him it was by faith that a person was saved, not by following the law. Again, Barnabas came to Paul's assistance in telling about the miraculous signs and wonders God had performed among the Gentile believers.

IMPRISONED!

Paul was imprisoned several times. In Philippi, God provided Silas to accompany him. In Rome, Epaphras and Luke were there. In Caesarea, the local believers visited him. Paul's need was expressed when he wrote to Timothy, "Do your best to come to me quickly, for Demas . . . has deserted me . . . Only Luke is with me. Get Mark and bring him with you, because he is helpful to me in my ministry" (2 Tim. 4:9–11 NIV).

The times of imprisonment were no short ventures. He spent more than two years in jail in Caesarea, and more than two years in the Roman prison (Acts 28:30). Companionship would prove to be an essential component to the success or failure of Paul's ministry.

THREATS AND CONSTANT DANGER

The constant threat of the Judaizers was something Paul could not have handled alone. Their never-ending attacks required constant vigilance and caused Paul to be on the move from town to town, ever watchful of those who sought to destroy him.

On at least three occasions there were plots to take Paul's life. Each time, believers foiled the plans, saving Paul's life. One time he was let down from the city wall of Damascus at night (Acts 9:25). Another time he was hurried out of Jerusalem to Caesarea and sent to Tarsus (Acts 9:30). God allowed Paul's nephew to overhear a scheme to kill Paul, which brought enhanced Roman security (Acts 23:16). Without the keen hearing and quick action of Paul's fellow believers, he would not have survived.

The one time when Paul's adversaries stoned him, dragged him out of the city, and left him for dead in Lystra (Acts 14:19), his friends could not stop it. But we have a beautiful picture of their devotion to him. The Scripture says, "But the disciples formed a circle around him, and he got up and went back to town. The next day he went on with Barnabas to Derbe" (Acts 14:20 ISV). The disciples gathered around Paul. They formed a circle of prayer and encouragement. Something incredible happened that day, for he was able to travel the road to Derbe in the morning. There were many times when Paul's colleagues, companions, fellow workers, and fellow believers "formed a circle around him," whether it was through prayer, sending money for his needs, opening their homes to him, caring for his wounds, or just by living lives that demonstrated the power of God in them.

> **Without the keen hearing and quick action of Paul's fellow believers, he would not have survived.**

PAUL'S TRUSTED MESSENGERS

One of Paul's greatest needs was for messengers that he could send to churches to encourage and exhort them. Among others, Paul sent Timothy to Philippi, Corinth, and Thessalonica; Tychicus to Ephesus and Colosse; and Titus to Ephesus, Corinth, and Crete. With such long distances to travel, it was difficult for Paul to have a personal presence in the churches. But his trusted emissaries, ambassadors in the faith, could assist in the preservation and discipling of new converts and in establishing them in their faith.

> I did not take advantage of you through any of the men I sent you, did I? I encouraged Titus to visit you, and I sent along with him the brother you know so well. Titus didn't take advantage of you, did he? We conducted ourselves with the same spirit, didn't we? We took the very same steps, didn't we? (2 Cor. 12:17–18 ISV)

That's why I sent Timothy to you. I love him like a son, and he is a faithful servant of the Lord. Timothy will tell you what I do to follow Christ and how it agrees with what I always teach about Christ in every church. (1 Cor. 4:17 CEV)

It is a testimony to the faithful care of Paul that, in the face of tremendous persecution and internal strife, there was very little defection from his churches compared to what we see today.

In the face of tremendous persecution and internal strife, there was very little defection from Paul's churches compared to what we see today.

FRIENDSHIP

Besides the need for faithful ministerial companions, Paul also had the basic human need for friendship. God provided friends like Aquila and his wife, Priscilla, as well as traveling companions, such as Silas and Timothy, Barnabas and Titus, and a host of others. His need is expressed in Acts 17:15 (NIV), where he "left . . . instructions for Silas and Timothy to join him as soon as possible," and in his letter to Timothy: "Do your best to come to me quickly . . . Only Luke is with me . . . do your best to get here before winter" (2 Tim. 4:9–11, 21 NIV).

God knew what needy times would come in the life of Paul, and He placed certain people around him for such times. His first imprisonment was one of the neediest times. Out of that time, a deep bonding developed between Paul and the church in Philippi. They continued to send people to help him, and they were a great encouragement. Their care would leave a lasting mark on his life. A woman named Lydia and Paul's own jailer both became lifelong supporters of Paul. They were his prayer partners and prayer warriors to undergird his ministry.

There are some whom God has richly blessed with wealth. Often He moves in their hearts to participate in His kingdom work by supporting various projects, outreach events, or servants who minister in Christ's name. Just as Jesus had those like Mary from Magdala (Luke 8:2–3), who shared from her possessions to take care of His needs, Paul, too, had faithful financial backers at different times in his life.

Lydia (Acts 16:14–15, 40), a Philippian businesswoman, was one whose heart was stirred when she listened to Paul, Silas, and John Mark. She strongly persuaded them to come to her house so she could hear more about the gospel of Christ. It was what she had been looking for, and she quickly became one of Paul's strongest supporters throughout his ministry.

After a riot ensued in Philippi over Paul's healing of a slave girl, Paul and his traveling companion, Silas, were imprisoned, stripped, and beaten. The Bible actually says they were "severely flogged" (Acts 16:23 NIV) and were thrown into the inner prison; their feet were locked into the stocks, and the key was all but thrown away. But even in prison, Paul and Silas were able to rejoice in the goodness of God. God responded by miraculously intervening, shaking the doors of the prison open and redeeming the life of a hardened jailer. It was to Lydia's house that they went when they were finally released.

Lydia's support did not stop there. Throughout the rest of Paul's journeys, money and goods kept coming from this little church in Philippi to sustain his ministry and to be an enormous encouragement to him personally:

> You Philippians also know that in the early days of the gospel, when I left Macedonia, no church participated with me in the matter of giving and receiving except for you. Even while I was in Thessalonica, you provided for my needs not once, but twice. I have been paid in full and have more than enough. I am fully supplied, now that I have received from Epaphroditus what you sent—a fragrant aroma, a sacrifice acceptable and pleasing to God. (Phil. 4:15–16, 18 ISV)

It all seems to have happened because Lydia opened her home and her heart to the things of God and wanted to participate in God's activity through Paul's life. There were numerous people scattered all over Asia Minor who had this same heart toward Paul. And Paul reciprocated the feeling, as he continually wrote back to communicate with his supporters and encouragers. We have no record or only slight references to many of Paul's letters.

COMPANIONS

Companions were not just colleagues, friends, or associates; they were much more. To Paul, his companions were indispensable fellow laborers for Christ. These were not casual acquaintances, nor were they relatives obligated to like him. These were people willing to die with him if necessary. In Philemon, Paul uses the terms *fellow soldier, fellow prisoner,* and *fellow laborer* (vv. 1–2, 23–24). Though there were often elements of discipling, training, partnering, and equipping of those with whom Paul ministered, their relationship went much deeper. The level of *koinonia* (fellowship or practical *agape* love) between Paul and his companions is what we hope every believer can achieve in his or her own ministry.

THE ROLE OF THE HOLY SPIRIT IN COMPANIONSHIP

Walking in harmony with the Spirit means He will live out His life through you. Several times in the Bible, God says that it is impossible for us to have love for others if we do not properly love Him first. This is because it is God who shows us what love truly is. Any love apart from God is only a sad imitation of what God can demonstrate in and through our lives toward others. In the same way, the Holy Spirit models for us what true companionship is like so that we can have this same type of companionship with others. Jesus knew full well that the assignment Paul had been given would require a very close relationship with His Spirit, and Jesus spent three years with Paul in Arabia helping him to understand this and to apply this in his own life (Gal. 1:15–20). The Holy Spirit as Paul's companion would prove to be the most significant aspect of Paul's ministry. For without the guiding, encouraging, protecting hand of God's Spirit, we would not have half of our New Testament writings nor the churches Paul established throughout Asia Minor.

Paul was right in the middle of it all. His desire was to establish churches, not just to evangelize the lost.

It was the Spirit of Christ who continually put Paul in touch with other believers and created the fellowship and supportive relationships Paul needed to fulfill his ministry mandate. This was one of the key factors in how God turned the Roman Empire upside down. Everywhere one went, believers were sprouting up. If one tried to stomp out one group, another more determined group sprang up. And Paul was right in the middle of it all. His desire was to establish churches, not just to evangelize the lost.

CHRIST AS COMPANION

During the three years Paul spent with Christ in the wilderness, Jesus was revealing to Paul what He planned to do to reach the Gentiles. Paul needed to join Christ in His plans for Asia Minor.

There was a time in Corinth when Paul needed reminding of the abiding presence of Christ in his life and work. Here Christ came to him in a vision and said, "Do not be afraid; keep on speaking, do not be silent. For I am with you, and no one is going to . . . harm you, because I have many people in this city" (Acts 18:9–10 NIV).

Christ later called Paul to Macedonia. There Paul met Lydia and established a church that would be a faithful donor to facilitate his ministry. God meant to reach the world through the Western cultures. Paul was to share the gospel with them; they would respond by taking the gospel to the rest of the world. Only in recent years have Eastern cultures begun sending missionaries en masse, a change from God's original intent.

PAUL ESTABLISHED PATTERNS AND USED STRATEGIES

There was a definite pattern and strategy to Paul's church-planting ministry. First, Paul preached with his companions in a new city, often starting at the synagogue or marketplace. As they gained converts, they gathered them together and discipled them, usually in the home of one of the believers. Next, Paul established some semblance of a church, in which he would then select elders and spiritual leaders to guide and stabilize it. Paul would then do his best to visit this church in the coming years or send his trusted representatives to encourage them and establish them in their faith and work.

He continued to foster relationships through the companions he sent, the letters he wrote, and most desirably, any personal visits he could make. He looked forward to receiving regular reports from them and keeping up with them through information given by those who had visited them on his behalf. The clear indication that they were constantly on his heart was the continuous intercessory prayer he made for them. For where your heart is, your prayers will be focused.

As I reflect back over my early ministry in Canada, many people come to mind who joined us in our work of planting and establishing churches. Some not only left all to join us, but also stayed and took out Canadian citizenship to better identify with us. They worked hard to lay a strong foundation for many who would be called into ministry through our efforts.

God sent some of His choicest servants to work with us over the years. Some of them sacrificed a great deal as they shared in helping us achieve our mission and were invaluable components in much of what God did through us. Others left us when the times got tough, choosing to go back home where they were more comfortable, to jobs that did not require so much sacrifice, or because they became discouraged quickly. Some of those who departed years ago, or who came to visit us in view of joining us and decided not to, have spoken with me years later to express their regret and sadness. They realized that God had planned to do much in our ministry, and they could have been a part of it, but chose another path instead.

God essentially calls His servants, both prominent and behind the scenes, to "walk together" in love and *koinonia* (partnership) with Him as He reaches out to a lost world. To enable this He puts it in their hearts to (1) receive companions He sends and (2) to be companions to others who are His servants. He does this both with individuals and with churches who are to be "partners" and companions with others in His kingdom.

These two verses are important to this study, and we will refer back to them throughout this book:

- "Truly, truly I tell you, the one who receives whomever I send receives me, and the one who receives me receives the one who sent me" (John 13:20 ISV).

- "The one who receives you receives me, and the one who receives me receives the one who sent me" (Matt. 10:40 ISV).

These verses are the heart of this book, because they encapsulate the essence of companionship: receiving the ones God sends us as though we are receiving Christ—and being Christ to others as we walk with them in companionship.

STUDY QUESTIONS

1. How God initiates your conversion may be His pacesetter for the rest of your life. Take a spiritual inventory of your conversion. What were the factors surrounding it? Remember, how God initiates you into His kingdom may have a great deal to do with how you will be used in His kingdom.

2. Who introduced you to the Lord? Was there something in your introduction to Christ that reveals God's plans for your life in ministry?

3. Suffering alone causes the need for companionship to be multiplied a hundredfold. Companionship during suffering is crucial. Suicide in God's people demonstrates that suffering alone should never take place. A church *must* be aware of the members of its body and partner with them in their suffering. Paul's suffering normally took place with companions who together faced imprisonment, beatings, flogging, and humiliation. Is there someone suffering emotionally or physically with whom God wants you to walk? How can your church or organization partner with such people?

4. Your relationship to Christ will determine the degree to which you have a servant's heart. It is a spontaneous result of God working in your life. It will affect how you receive companions and how you are a companion to others. How does your life reflect the servant heart of Christ?

5. There is a mentality among some pastors that when they leave a church and move on to the next one, they break all ties with the last one. These ministers sever bonds with those who have faithfully supported and prayed for them. Had Paul taken this attitude, many churches would have died. There is no individual church that has the ability to reach its entire city. Churches must work together with other churches God has placed in the city. To ignore God's other bodies of believers in a city is to ignore what God is doing. We are not created to work on our own, but together with God's people. How is it possible to continue a partnership with a former pastor?

6. Are you willing to be a servant, a colaborer, a companion to others, or must you always be in charge?

7. Describe God's purposed interdependence in Paul's life and how it is necessary in your own life.

TWO

THE REWARDS AND COST OF COMPANIONSHIP

ONE OF THE BEST PARTS of companionship is having someone to rejoice with when the successes come! Whether there is one other person or an entire team of people, each person does his best with his God-given skills and talents to achieve a goal that none of them could have managed on their own. Each one pays a price, and each shares in the glory as God brings the results.

There was an absolute uniqueness to Paul's call. He was to cross into the unknown, bringing the message across culture, language, geography, and religions. The magnitude of the assignment dictated the significance of his companions. Those who stay home and don't do much won't need companions to assist them. But the more demanding your role, the more critical your need for companions will be. Because God knows the assignments He has for His servants, He also knows the kind of companions they will need to accomplish their assignments.

In the early 1970s, Bill McLeod and I prayed earnestly with others for revival to come to our city of Saskatoon. We joined together in seeking God's will and asking His Spirit to fall on our city.

In 1972 we were able to see it come to pass. Together we rejoiced as scores of people came to Christ. I also made a covenant with Jerry Wortman to pray for the Native Indians in northern Saskatchewan, and we saw several preaching points eventually turned into churches. Len Koster and I prayed together and traveled the highways and back roads of Saskatchewan with a heart to see some churches planted in each of the towns that had no evangelical witness. Over the next twelve years we saw some thirty churches and missions planted around Saskatchewan and Manitoba. During my time in Vancouver when I served as director of missions for the Capilano Baptist Association, I worked with a group of committed servants of Christ (namely, Barbara McKenzie, Linda Hokit, and Renee O'Niel) on the 1986 World's Fair. We labored greatly together in planning, organizing, praying, and facilitating as God led. Together with other partnering organizations, God brought some twenty thousand professions of faith during that one event.

In God's design for ministry, the sower and the reaper celebrate together when the harvest comes in. Neither one's work is more important than the other's. And both get to enjoy the fruit of their labor. John 4:36 says it plainly: "He who sows and he who reaps . . . rejoice together." This is so true in God's kingdom. First Corinthians 3:6 (NIV) shows this principle in action: "I planted the seed, Apollos watered it, but God made it grow." Each one of us has a role to play, each does his part, and God puts it all together to bring glory to Himself. The advantage of companionship is that, by working together, you get to experience the benefits of both your own expertise and work *and* the skill of those working with you. It is amazing to see what God can do when He puts particular people together for an assignment He has given them.

There are plenty of examples of people who worked alone in ministry in the Old Testament, particularly the prophets. Elijah was one of God's most amazing prophets, who demonstrated God's incredible power. He had no companions to walk with him during the major part of his ministry, and when he felt threatened by Jezebel, he ran off in self-pity, wanting to die. "I alone am left," he said, "and they seek to take my life" (1 Kings 19:10).

God saw Elijah's heart was weak, so He put Elisha with him as a companion until the end.

Jonah is one of the sad stories of what can happen to a man of God who is alone in ministry: "I am angry enough to die," he sniveled (4:9). His story ends on such a pathetic note, with him sitting alone under a dead vine.

But there were also examples of God's servants who had some great ministry teams. God gave Moses several companions. Aaron was the spiritual leader, Joshua was the military leader, and Moses was the general leader. The companions played different roles, but they all entered into the rewards of the journey. Aaron stood with Moses before Pharaoh and was the spokesperson. He had the relationship with the people, whereas Moses had grown up with the Egyptians and had been out of the country several decades. Probably the best picture of companionship was when the ransomed tribes fought their first battle with Amalek in Rephidim; Moses stood on a hill overlooking the scene of the conflict with the rod of God in his outstretched hand. On this occasion he was attended by Aaron, his brother, and Hur, his brother-in-law, who held up his wearied hands till Joshua and the chosen warriors of Israel gained the victory (Ex. 17:8–13). They all won the battle together, each one doing his part.

There is a great example of teamwork in 1 Samuel 14, where Jonathan, the son of Saul, with the young man who bore his armor, went down to the Philistines and wreaked havoc on their army. The two went side by side into battle and killed twenty men between them. The key was best expressed when Prince Jonathan said, "It may be that the LORD will work for us. For nothing restrains the LORD from saving by many or by few" (1 Sam. 14:6).

Perhaps the most oft-identified example of companionship is that of David and Jonathan. They had a brotherly love for each other that defied even the king's wrath. First Samuel 18:1 says, "David and Jonathan became best friends. Jonathan thought as much of David as he did of himself."

Jonathan risked his life for his friend, despite the fact that his own father sought to kill David at all costs.

Jonathan risked his life for his friend, despite the fact that his own father sought to kill David at all costs.

Jeremiah teamed up with his faithful scribe, Baruch (32:12–16, 36:4–8, 45:1), to record many oracles to be read to the leaders of his day. On one occasion, the king had each page of the document burned in front of him as he read it out loud. This would have been more than a little intimidating. But together they brought the Word of God to a people desperate for repentance and revival.

Though the Old Testament is rich with examples of companionship, it is the New Testament that serves as the best illustration for the church today as we follow Christ and continue His ministry until He returns. In fact, Christ Himself was given twelve men to serve under Him and with Him during His three years of earthly ministry. The Bible says, "He loved them to the very end" (John 13:1 CEV). Among them, He chose three to be His closest friends. One of them, John, was even known as the one "whom Jesus loved" (John 13:23) because of his close friendship with Him. I have often wondered if it was this special bond that allowed John to live the longest of all the apostles and to be given the special revelation that concludes the Scriptures.

JESUS HAD COMPANIONS

The Bible records that Peter, James, and John, these three only, were with Jesus on three occasions: (1) when He brought Jairus's daughter to life; (2) on the Mount of Transfiguration; and (3) when He prayed in the Garden of Gethsemane.

When Jesus called Peter, He gave him a net full of fishes that was too large for him to carry alone. So Peter called his companions to come and help him. I wonder if Jesus was watching to see who his companions were before Peter called them. Isn't it interesting to see that two sets of brothers were also called as disciples? Two brothers united can be much stronger than two strangers working together because of their history, their knowledge of each other's strengths and weaknesses, and their deep love for one another. These became Christ's companions.

Jesus was also granted deep friendships with a nearby family in Bethany. Of their relationship, John said, "Jesus loved Martha and her sister and [their brother]" (John 11:5).

THE POWER OF TWO

There were some people Jesus could always count on for support and encouragement when everyone else around Him sought to trap Him, refute Him, slander Him, or manipulate Him in some way. They would be His lifelong companions. In Jesus' wisdom, He sent His disciples out to surrounding villages two by two (Mark 6:17). He knew the support they could be to one another. (Also, in a more practical sense, their chances of fending off robbers were greatly enhanced by traveling in pairs.)

In God's wisdom and perfect plan, we find a certain role reversal after Christ's resurrection between Him and His disciples. While on earth, the disciples followed Christ and walked with Him. But after His death and resurrection, He walked with them and then sent the Holy Spirit to be their helper, guide, and lifelong companion.

I marvel at Dr. Billy Graham and his two lifelong companions, George Beverly Shea and Cliff Barrows. What a tremendous team they have been and what an extraordinary impact they have had by working together for more than five decades! Dr. Graham said, "I've been listening to Bev Shea sing for more than 50 years, and I would still rather hear him sing than anyone else I know" (www.billygraham.org/Biographies). Music has played a significant role in the Billy Graham Crusades, and the teamwork of music and program director Cliff Barrows and singer George Beverly Shea has enabled them to share the gospel around the globe.

Among the towns where we started Canadian mission churches, there were none where someone had not already been praying for a church to be established: Ben Bonney in Leroy; Cliff Scott in Prince Albert; T. V. George (Sotnekow) prayed for more than fifteen years in Allan; and Doris Turner prayed for twenty-three years in Kyle and saw nineteen adults at our first Bible study. In every case, God had been preparing people to partner with us before we had any idea we would ever plant a church. We came alongside them as companions and friends and helped them accomplish what God had given them a heart's desire to do. When a church is established, the companions can all rejoice together. We see Paul encouraging God's people in Cyprus, in Rome, and many other locations as he came to their aid, helping them to become established and strengthened as churches.

For fourteen years Bill and Maxine Shadle brought a group of students from Denton, Texas, up to Canada to assist our struggling churches and new missions with church building and renovations projects, Backyard Bible clubs, outreach choir concerts, and much more. Each successive year that they came back, they were able to see the rewards for their efforts as a new, growing congregation met in facilities they had built or renovated. Their reward was seeing scores of people come to Christ in places they had painted, roofed, insulated, and constructed. And all of this, thanks to a team of two.

We really want to emphasize the fact that it was God who initiated the pattern of sending out by twos, as He set apart Paul and Barnabas *together* in Antioch (Acts 13:2). It was a pattern that Paul would adhere to throughout his ministry. This was established by divine decree, not by a mission strategist. Not all had the assignment Paul had to take the gospel to the Gentiles. But many could be friends and companions to Paul and participate together as God gave "the increase" (1 Cor. 3:7).

Every pastor, missionary, ministry worker, and Christian ought to anticipate that God may give him a companion, not only for his benefit, but for the benefit of the companion as well. I don't think many people realize just how much Paul invested in Timothy or exactly what impact Barnabas had on Paul's life. Neither can we overestimate the influence Jesus had on the lives of His disciples. This begs the question, who is following in your footsteps in ministry? Are you investing in someone with whom you can rejoice together in

> **Not all had the assignment Paul had to take the gospel to the Gentiles. But many could be friends and companions to Paul.**

the fruit God brings? Who is standing with you, committed to be with you through all situations you face? Associate staff, given by God, can fill this role for pastors. Assistants can help teachers. Your colleagues can be your helpers and companions in ministry and even follow in your steps after you are gone.

PAUL HAD COMPANIONS

Each Companion Has a Unique Characteristic to Bring to Your Life

Every companion God brought to Paul was equipped with special character traits and abilities that would be needed in Paul's life and ministry. We sometimes look at the skills a person has rather than the character behind them. Paul knew that it would not be great oratory or administrative skills that would help a person stand under persecution; it would be character. Looking at the various companions who accompanied Paul, we see that each possessed unique attributes and provided Paul with particular insights and encouragements that would carry him through both the difficult times and the good times he would encounter on his travels. Let's look briefly at some of the companions God gave Paul and what they added to his life and ministry. We will learn more about these and many others in chapters 4 and 5.

SILAS

Silas means "wood." Besides being one-half of a great singing duet in prison (Acts 16:25), Silas's skills were those of an evangelist (2 Cor. 1:19). He was also a prophet who was recognized by the churches both in Jerusalem and in Antioch. More than anyone else, he was a steadfast helper during severe trials and was one who could strengthen, encourage, and establish other believers. After Paul's death, Silas continued the ministry of Paul, working with the apostle Peter to carry letters of encouragement to the churches. Silas's moral courage in the face of persecution and imprisonment steadied Paul's resolve and personal convictions at a time when they could have faltered.

BARNABAS

His name means "patient encourager." The apostles named Barnabas "son of encouragement" (*prophecy* or *exhortation*) because of his character and behavior. He was the gentle giant among the brethren. Barnabas sought out Paul in Tarsus and brought him to the church in Jerusalem because he saw great potential in him. Then he took Paul as his assistant on the first missionary journey, giving him his first taste of missionary life, and helped him establish the strategy for church planting. He was also at Paul's side when mob justice sought Paul's life through stoning. Barnabas's service to Paul was indispensable as he laid the foundations and initial encouragement for Paul to fulfill his God-given mandate to take the gospel to the Gentiles.

LUKE

Luke was more than a physician; he was a documenter of the activities of Paul and an eyewitness to what God did through him. As a Gentile convert of Paul's, he would have provided Paul with some insight into the culture of non-Jews. Some believe Luke to be the brother of Titus, a young pastor (2 Cor. 8:18–23). His medical knowledge certainly would have come in handy when dealing with Paul's many beatings, whipping, imprisonments, etc. But above all, Luke seems to have been a close friend and traveling companion of Paul's. He accompanied him on several missionary adventures, including his last trip to Rome. Luke provided medical attention, encouragement, and friendship, as well as cross-cultural understanding to Paul's ministry.

TITUS

Titus means "honorable." He was a trusted emissary sent by Paul to address immorality in the Corinthian church, even delivering Paul's second letter to the Corinthians. Paul also trusted Titus to establish the church in Crete. He was one of the few companions of Paul's to receive a personal letter from Paul.

Paul was often limited in his movements. This and the fact that there were great distances to cover and many new churches to encourage and establish made it necessary for representatives like Titus to go on Paul's behalf. What a great relief it was to be able to send one who was trusted and competent to minister to these new believers.

AQUILA AND PRISCILLA

This young couple, fellow tent makers, provided Paul with a home away from home. Aquila and Priscilla were one of very few couples mentioned by Paul in his writings, and I can imagine the home life they offered would have been a welcome respite to this weary traveler. They also offered their home as the meeting place for churches in several cities. The Bible records that they accompanied Paul to Ephesus and took on the responsibility of instructing Apollos according to Paul's teachings. Paul makes no secret as to their importance to him personally, as he mentions them in his letters to the churches.

TIMOTHY

The name *Timothy* means "honoring God," and Paul lists him in the greetings of six of his letters (1 and 2 Corinthians, Philemon, 1 and 2 Thessalonians, and Philippians). He was Paul's *son in the faith* and became a young pastor in whom Paul could invest his life. Paul became a companion to Timothy as he imparted his wisdom and encouragement to this young man and constantly encouraged him to be strong. It was Paul's hope that young Timothy would carry on his work when he was gone. He is the only individual to receive two personal letters from Paul and to be directly discipled by him (Phil. 2:19–23). He may also have been one of the few on whom Paul directly laid his hands to anoint him for ministry (2 Tim. 1:6). Timothy became a trusted ambassador to the churches (1 Cor. 4:17) and provided Paul with a vision for the future. (Paul knew that it would be men like Timothy who would take the newly founded churches to their next stage of growth.)

JOHN MARK

"Get Mark and bring him with you, for he is useful to me" (2 Tim. 4:11). Mark was likely converted under Peter's ministry in Jerusalem. He was asked to accompany his cousin (or uncle) Barnabas and the apostle Paul as a helper on their first missionary journey. He lost the respect of Paul when he left them at Perga to go home. By the end of Paul's ministry, however, Mark had earned Paul's admiration and had become very useful to Paul in ministry. John Mark had turned out to be a hard worker and a faithful servant. He began his relationship with Paul as a helper. At the end of Paul's ministry, Mark again is seen as a much-needed helper to Paul.

God brought many others alongside Paul throughout his ministry, as encouragers, coworkers, fellow prisoners, and evangelists, each adding something new as he or she came. I have no doubt that among them were great storytellers for those nights spent around campfires, men who were logistically astute, some who had special contacts in various cities, others who could prepare food, and still more who were good at helping Paul refine and focus his messages as he preached from city to city. Paul not only learned to trust his companions, but he also learned to depend on them.

This has been true in my life also. God was faithful to send me quality companions throughout my ministry, each one bringing a special talent or insight for ministry. Robert Cannon added the dimension of student ministry through which 180 college students were baptized and nearly 100 were called into ministry. Jack Connor added stability to our ministry and helped us address the needs of the Native Indian community in his area. Jack also challenged me to press everything up against the Scriptures. Len Koster, my coworker in church planting, dared me to see the positive side of everything that could easily have been seen as negative. He was such a delightful personality, and his winsome smile and laugh were so disarming and very encouraging to me. Len was definitely a Barnabas to me, and I deeply miss him to this day.

John Cunningham, a fellow pastor in Canada, challenged me to have a shepherd's heart simply by his example in how he ministered to others. T. W. Hunt, Minette Drumright, Avery Willis, and I prayed regularly together as we were assigned the task of leading our national convention into a prayer focus. We were accountability partners to one another and were responsible to guide the convention for Bold Mission Prayer Thrust. Avery experienced the Indonesian revival and helped me see a vision of what a national revival looked like. Minette's confidence in prayer was an incredible inspiration to me personally. I greatly appreciated T. W.'s strong grasp of the biblical nature and pattern of prayer. The four of us met in various ways for many years until God began to take each of us in a different direction.

When God brings companions about you, seek to understand how God has equipped them to add dimensions to your life and ministry that are needed to complement what is lacking. My own life/ministry to this day is the product of many faithful companions that God provided to me.

COMPANIONSHIP IS NOT NECESSARILY MENTORING

Mentoring is most often a unidirectional relationship. The mentor teaches the trainee. The trainee absorbs as much as possible from the mentor so that he will be able to go on his own at some point. It is similar to a master-and-disciple relationship. To be a companion is to be a *partner* in ministry. Both have skills; both have roles; both have been equipped and gifted by God for mutual edification.

Whereas the beginning relationship between Paul and Timothy appears to have been similar to that of a mentor and a trainee, it became much more as they served together. Paul watched for young men in whom he could invest his life and whom he could encourage in the faith. Many different names of traveling companions are mentioned, all coming from different regions where Paul had traveled. To Paul, mentoring was only one component of the discipleship strategy. This was not an intellectual exercise; it was an act of giving his life to others to help them become God's servants and his fellow workers. I doubt that Paul gave classes on theology, church planting, or eschatology. Instead, he would take the young believers with him and let them watch him as he preached, taught, healed, encouraged, and demonstrated his faith. How else could he say, "Follow my example, as I follow the example of Christ" (1 Cor. 11:1 NIV) unless they had opportunity to walk with him and observe his life?

But Paul had no intention of being a hero or an idol to the younger Christians. He continuously directed attention away from himself and onto Christ, his Lord and Master: "For to me, to live is Christ" (Phil. 1:21). We will address this more fully in chapter 3.

Paul watched for young men in whom he could invest his life and whom he could encourage in the faith.

An interesting outcome of Luke's and Mark's companionship with Paul was perhaps the writing of two Gospels, in addition to the coauthorship of Paul's letters to Philemon and the Colossians. As Paul is well-known for his many letters, he may have been an inspiration to these companions to write as well. Both men spent considerable time with Paul and had many opportunities to interview and converse with the other apostles and eyewitnesses. We can speculate that Luke and Mark might have talked together and determined that one (Luke) should write a detailed account with a focus on the Gentile audience and the other (Mark) would try to get a simple version of the story of Christ out as quickly as possible.

PAUL MODELED COMPANIONSHIP

It is nearly impossible to have strong companions unless you are also willing to *be* a companion. God could trust Paul with companions because he had demonstrated his ability to be one first. "With the same measure that you use, it will be measured back to you," says Luke 6:38. I believe that Paul was haunted by his past throughout his life and that his early opposition to the Christian church motivated him to do whatever he could to encourage believers and strengthen the body. He showed what true companionship is like as he invested in other lives and in all the churches. Paul lived his own instructions: "Do nothing out of selfish ambition or vain conceit, but in humility consider others better than yourselves. Each of you should look not only to your own interests, but also to the interests of others" (Phil. 2:3–4 NIV). He constantly challenged them to rise to God's assignment for them. He encouraged them to use their full potential in Christ to spread the gospel message and to be salt and light where God had placed them. He wrote letters of instruction and encouragement as well as letters of rebuke.

Paul also sent people to encourage churches, to direct them, and to check up on his investment in their lives (Eph. 6:21). Mark, Timothy, Silas, Apollos, Titus, and Tychicus were all sent by Paul with letters, encouragement, and directives to return to him with a report on how the churches were getting along. In addition, over and over we see that Paul's companions also sent their greetings to the churches (Rom. 16:21–24, Phil. 4:21). The adage is true: "A man that hath friends, must show himself to be friendly" (Prov. 18:24 KJV).

The Corinthian church was particularly troublesome to Paul. That is why he had to visit them "for the third time" (2 Cor. 12:14 NIV). He said of them, "I will very gladly spend for you everything I have . . . I have not been a burden to you" (vv. 15–16 NIV).

To the Ephesians Paul did not stop "from declaring unto you the whole counsel of God" (Acts 20:27 ASV). He also spent a great deal of time warning them about those who wished their demise. "I know that after I leave, savage wolves will come in among you . . . so be on your guard!" (Acts 20:29–31 NIV). At Paul's core, I have no doubt that he was happy to have the opportunity to demonstrate the kind of love Christ spoke of in John 15:13: "Greater love has no one than this, than to lay down one's life for his friends."

You cannot read a letter of Paul's without getting the sense that he acknowledged those who were important to him. The very fact that in six of his letters he mentioned Timothy and others as sending the letter proves that he was in no way self-serving or desirous of recognition. He was very aware of the contribution so many others were making in ministry with him. Paul also found great encouragement from his friends and coworkers as they remained faithful to Christ. "Your love has given me great joy and encouragement, because you, brother, have refreshed the hearts of the saints . . . Prepare a guest room for me . . . I hope to be restored to you in answer to your prayers" (Philem. 1:7, 22 NIV). Acts 20:36 is a very moving scene: "When he had said these things, he knelt down and prayed with them all. Then they wept freely, and fell on Paul's neck and kissed him, sorrowing most of all for the words which he spoke, that they would see his face no more." On more than one occasion, tears were shed at his departure by church members and by fellow laborers in the kingdom. I often wonder if one of the reasons Paul had deep, enduring relationships with those he met was because he was never guaranteed to see them again and had to make the most of every friendship while there was time.

Arrogance, pride, and selfish ambition have no place within companionship.

It is so sad to see some Christian leaders today who refuse to follow the advice of their God-given companions and advisors and not only lose respect within their community because of it, but never realize what their lives and ministry could have been had they listened. What is even more troubling is that these very leaders are held up as examples by those who want to follow in their footsteps and use them as excuses for continuing in sin. Arrogance, pride, and selfish ambition have no place within companionship. God will place people around us to help us avoid these very things.

THE COST OF COMPANIONSHIP

"But the Lord said to Ananias, 'Go! This man is my chosen instrument to carry my name before the Gentiles and their kings and before the people of Israel. . . . He must suffer for my name'" (Acts 9:15–16 NIV).

Paul was called to ministry, and he was called to suffer. Being a companion to Paul also meant sharing in his suffering. He was not hesitant to suggest that suffering would be common and shared by all true believers. Paul wrote to Timothy, his son in the faith, "All who desire to live godly in Christ Jesus will suffer persecution" (2 Tim. 3:12).

A Jewish synagogue ruler named Sosthenes was one such sufferer who paid the price for supporting Paul in Corinth. When a riotous Corinthian crowd (Acts 18:17) realized it could not prosecute Paul, they grabbed Sosthenes and beat him up in front of the court while the governor watched. Among Paul's companions, Silas was put in a Philippian jail; Barnabas faced the rioting crowds in Ephesus; Timothy was imprisoned; and Epaphras shared a prison cell with Paul in Rome. On another occasion, a mob "rushed to Jason's house in search of Paul and Silas in order to bring them out to the crowd. But when they did not find them, they dragged Jason and some other brothers before the city officials, shouting" (Acts 17:5–9 NIV). Though they were released, the experience must have been frightening.

Certainly Christ's disciples also paid a heavy price for being His companions. John was exiled to Patmos, and all were martyred, beginning with James (Acts 12:2). Many other followers in the New Testament suffered the same fate, including Paul. Here are some of Paul's writings regarding suffering:

- "In fact, when we were with you, we kept telling you that we would be persecuted. And it turned out that way, as you well know" (1 Thess. 3:4 NIV).

- "Do not be ashamed to testify about our Lord, or ashamed of me his prisoner. But join with me in suffering for the gospel, by the power of God" (2 Tim. 1:8 NIV).

- "I endure everything for the sake of the elect" (2 Tim. 2:10 NIV).
- "I now rejoice in my sufferings for you, and fill up in my flesh what is lacking in the afflictions of Christ, for the sake of His body, which is the church" (Col. 1:24).

To the Corinthian church, Paul reluctantly shared a litany of hardships that he endured for the cause of Christ. He listed them almost as a matter of fact, as though they were expected: imprisoned at least four times, flogged, given forty-nine lashes five times, beaten by rods three times, stoned, shipwrecked three times, spent a night and day in the open sea, ran from bandits, forded rivers, gone without sleep many times, gone hungry and thirsty, been exposed to cold, and been denied clothing.

We should remember that for most of these events, he was not alone. There were companions with him who often had to endure the same things because they were together. But even in his sufferings, Paul added a note of encouragement to those who felt his pain and prayed for his safety: "I ask you, therefore, not to be discouraged because of my sufferings for you, which are your glory" (Eph. 3:13 NIV).

> A man's sin can often affect his whole family. In the same way, a companion can be caught up in the consequences of a leader's sins.

THE SINS OF A LEADER CAN COST THE COMPANIONS MUCH

Just as companions may have to endure sufferings as a part of their companionship, they may also share in the penalty for their leader's wrongdoing. Aaron died because of Moses' sin and rebellious heart (Num. 20). Both Moses *and* Aaron paid the consequences, dying in the mountains before their people entered the promised land. Young David was forced to deal with the disobedience of King Saul, often having to run for his life. A man's sin can often affect his whole family. In the same way, a companion can be caught up in the consequences of a leader's sins.

During these times, trusting God will be crucial, as it is God who defends the cause of the righteous and protects the reputations of those who serve Him faithfully. These may be extremely difficult periods for the companion, not to mention incredibly disappointing. But they will also be times of great need in the life of the leader. A companion who is more interested in his reputation than in the survival of his leader may abandon the leader at this critical time. But a godly companion will want to help the leader walk through the "valley of the shadow of death" (Ps. 23:4) and to repentance and restoration with his family and ministry.

A difficult truth to remember when the one with whom you are walking falls into sin is that God brought you to this person for a reason. To run away or abandon your leader could be an act of disobedience to God. In what ways could God use you to encourage that person? What is it that God wants *you* to learn?

Unfortunately, hundreds of companions have left the ministry altogether because of how they were treated by sinful pastors, carnal deacons, or ungodly church leadership. The sin of a leader can have a tremendous impact not only on his own ministry, but on the ministries of so many others around him.

Happily, none of Paul's companions had to face the consequences of Paul's sin. There were times when he was upset, discouraged, lonely, and perhaps a little harsh, but as far as the Scriptures tell us, he stayed on the path of faithfulness throughout his ministry. He did his best to never act in any way that would give cause for accusation or ridicule. To the Thessalonians he wrote, "My dear friends, you surely haven't forgotten our hard work and hardships. You remember how night and day we struggled to make a living, so that we could tell you God's message without being a burden to anyone. Both you and God are witnesses that we were pure and honest and innocent in our dealings with you followers of the Lord" (1 Thess. 2:9–10 CEV). Can the same be said of you?

STUDY QUESTIONS

1. Identify the unique characteristics and abilities your companions have brought to your life.

2. How have you personally benefited from companionship?

3. In what ways has companionship cost you personally? How have others paid a price to be your companions (your family, staff members, coworkers)?

4. In mentoring, one gives his or her time; in companionship, one gives his or her life. Have you been involved in a mentoring relationship when God really wanted you to be a companion to that person? Describe it.

5. Take a moment to read through the list of companions in this chapter and what they added to Paul's ministry. Can you identify people whom God has brought to your life that have functioned in similar ways?

6. If you are functioning alone in ministry, why do you think that is? Is it because you have not seen the companions God has brought, or could it be because you did not approve of those God has brought to you? Sometimes God does not send us what we want, but what we need.

7. John 4:36 says, "He who sows and he who reaps [will] rejoice together." In what ways have you seen sowing and reaping together happen in your own life?

8. Do you see things differently from before your companions influenced you? How?

THREE

PAUL NURTURED
RELATIONSHIPS

AS WE STUDY THE LIFE OF PAUL and the many letters he wrote to both churches and individuals, we notice just how much he loved people. On several occasions Paul told his friends that he had been praying night and day for them (1 Thess. 3:10; 2 Tim. 1:3), bringing them before God's throne of grace. This was not a requirement for an apostle; this was an act of a devoted friend and companion toward those he cared for. The sacrifices he made for believers were done willingly and demonstrated the extent to which he was willing to go to nurture the relationships God had given him.

Paul was a very influential person among believers. Yet he did not abuse his authority by demanding that believers comply with his wishes. Instead, with humility, love, and much prayer, he was able to show them the truth in such a way that they willingly followed it. I am amazed that he never used his weight and experience as a weapon against errant believers, but rather maintained a degree of humility that is rarely seen in our churches today. Paul wrote to the believers in Ephesus, "[I] am less than the least of all the saints" (Eph. 3:8). I believe he truly knew what it meant to be the recipient of God's abundant grace and to live under God's authority. He presented it so clearly to the Ephesians: "For by grace you have been saved through faith, and that not of yourselves; it is the gift of God, not of works, lest anyone should boast. For we are His workmanship, created in Christ Jesus for good works, which God prepared beforehand that we should walk in them" (Eph. 2:8–10).

His heart's desire was to draw folks to Christ in love rather than to drive them by his authority. Paul did not seek to develop his *own* kingdom; he developed God's kingdom. Though Paul was appointed as a discipler among God's people, he allowed the churches to be free to follow Christ as the head of His church. He was a strong leader, but also was a preeminent servant. As he grew in Christ, so did his desire to serve Christ and encourage His church: "When the riot was over, Paul sent for the followers and encouraged them. He then told them good-by and left for Macedonia. As he traveled from place to place, he encouraged the followers with many messages" (Acts 20:1–2 CEV). The more he was around God's people, the more indebted to them he became. Perhaps this is why he so effectively demonstrated servant leadership right to the end of his ministry.

Charles Spurgeon, a strong, highly respected preacher and leader, took time to establish a college for those who were called but were not able to manage university for various reasons. He made a way to provide them with training as preachers while they took care of their families and other obligations. He invested in the lives of young preachers and, through his prolific writing, inspired countless others. Four or five of my Blackaby relatives attended this college, and some of them received the small living stipend he presented to those with little income. What an example of a servant leader and an investor in the kingdom of God.

DIFFERENT KINDS OF RELATIONSHIPS

Paul had many levels of relationships with people. He had thousands of acquaintances, many friends, but fewer companions. There are different heights of commitment and obligation, depending on the category of relationship one has. I believe the bond the Holy Spirit creates between believers plays an important role in bringing mere acquaintances into the realm of companionship, but it takes time for that to happen. Paul could not trust a friend with the same important task with which he could trust his companions. Companionship requires a level of trust, commitment, loyalty, and love that no other relationship has. This is nowhere more evident than in the lifelong companionship between a husband and a wife. It is important to be able to identify and distinguish between various levels of relationships when working in ministry. Here are a few distinctions:

ACQUAINTANCES

Calling someone an acquaintance usually implies that one has a superficial knowledge of a person. Most of the time an acquaintance is merely a person you know, but know little about. An acquaintance may know your reputation or a few things about you but may not have the time to be a meaningful part of your life. Sometimes an acquaintance is more interested in telling you about himself and about how you can help him achieve his goals than he is in getting to know you personally. It grieves me when this happens.

I have traveled in ninety-six countries and have visited with some of His most faithful saints, who are doing incredible things in ministry with God. Still, I am always amazed that I can spend more than an hour in conversation with certain individuals and never once will they ask a single question about what God is doing in my life or through His people around the world. Some people

> Looking at people according to their status, reputations, or influence will prevent one from being a godly companion. Instead, we should always see one another as coworkers and fellow servants under a common Lord.

are so tunnel-visioned that they will only consider befriending those who will help them in their own little world.

Many have befriended me for the sole purpose of having me endorse their books, serve on their advisory board, or act as their reference, but never once offered to be an encouragement or support to me personally. They remind me of Simon of Samaria, who followed after Philip and the apostles and offered them money so that he could have their same powers (Acts 8:9–24). In other words, an acquaintance may sometimes come with an ulterior motive.

I have encountered people who were preoccupied with my perceived reputation or the influence they think I may have rather than with who I am and what God has called me to do. They are often either intimidated by me or enthralled simply because of what they have heard. I am ever astonished when, after spending time with such people, they say, "You are a pretty ordinary person. I didn't think I would be able to relate to you because of all you have done." Looking at people according to their status, reputations, or influence will prevent one from being a godly companion. Instead, we should always see one another as coworkers and fellow servants under a common Lord in the kingdom of God.

FRIENDS

There are various levels of friendship. At the lower level are those who may be related to you or have regular contact with you but do not sense an obligation or desire to walk with you in difficult circumstances. They do not have a high degree of loyalty because their other interests take precedence. (Demas was one such person. Paul said of him in 2 Timothy 4:10, "Because he loved this world, [he] has deserted me.") Christ speaks of a level of friendship that goes much deeper: "No longer do I call you servants, for a servant does not know what his master is doing; but I have called you friends, for all things that I heard from My Father I have made known to you" (John 15:15). Proverbs talks about deep friendships also: "There is a friend who sticks closer than a brother" (18:24). And the apostle John described the kind of friendship Christ demonstrated toward us: "No one shows greater love than when he lays down his life for his friends" (John 15:13 ISV).

Paul had many deep friendships with believers in several cities. Some opened their homes to him, others prayed diligently for him, some worked with him in ministry, and a few spent time in jail with him. Paul was so grateful to God for the friends He allowed him to have. It was the love of such friends that brought him much joy and comfort in times of distress.

PARTNERS

Partners have a common interest and shared goals and sometimes have major personal investments in you, your company, or your ministry. They know enough about your character and background to trust you and to work with you. They are willing to sacrifice (to a point) with you to achieve your common goals, but their interest is more in achieving the goal than in your life personally.

Often partners can be with you for a particular time in your life, but leave when other projects come up or when their assignment is over. I place Apollos in this category. There is no indication that Apollos ever spent much time with Paul, and there is no clear evidence that he traveled with him. But he was a gifted preacher/orator and a hard worker in the common cause of Christ. There wasn't the degree of investment in each other's life that is a key component of companionship. Paul endorsed Apollos and commended him to the brethren, but Apollos was of his own mind, and Paul was not able to convince him to travel to Corinth to encourage that church. Apollos's loyalty was without question to Christ, but he did not have any debt to Paul that he should immediately respond to Paul's request.

In the days of church planting in Canada, there were many who partnered with us to build churches and encourage congregations. Churches regularly sent financial gifts for pastoral support, for building projects, and for special events. One kind woman even purchased a school bus for us to use in our mission efforts! Others sent Sunday school materials for new churches, choral music for beginning choirs, and library books for the Christian training center. Some brought college groups to lead vacation Bible schools, youth retreats, and college outreach events. These folks partnered with us in our ministry and were a tremendous encouragement to us, but they were not able to make the long-term investments that companionship requires.

COMPANIONS

Companions have the key component of *koinonia* in their relationship, that combination of deep affection, partnership, fellowship, and willingness to sacrifice for one another that is so rarely seen today. They have a clear understanding that their love for God is to be expressed in their love for others and withhold nothing in the relationship to achieve that expression. A companion's bond of love and commitment can be lifelong and very significant at different points in your life.

Companionship leaves a mark on you for the rest of your life, for you will be different because of the relationship.

Look at the depth of relationship Paul had with the believers in Ephesus: "And saying these things, kneeling, he prayed with them all. And there was much weeping of all, and falling on the neck of Paul, they ardently kissed him, grieving most of all over the word which he had spoken, that they should see his face no more. And they went with him to the ship" (Acts 20:36–38 MKJV). They were heartbroken over his departure

46

and because it was the last time they would see him. Companionship leaves a mark on you for the rest of your life, for you will be different because of the relationship.

I have to admit that at each church we have served, there have been many tears when God called us to follow Him to another place of service. Our hearts broke over having to release dear brothers and sisters into the care of other pastors who would follow us, hoping that they would be treated with the same love and affection we felt toward them. When you minister together, sacrifice together, experience God's blessings as one, and collectively grow in Christ, your love naturally grows and deepens for one another. This is the natural outcome of godly companionship. If and when God leads companions to part ways, it is as though part of your heart is taken from you, and there is little consolation except in the knowledge that one day you will meet again together with your Lord.

Brother Yun, one of China's first house church leaders, suffered prolonged torture and imprisonment for his faith. God was able to accomplish much in his life, bringing many hundreds of people to Christ. Yun greatly valued his God-given companions and spoke of Xu Yongze as "my dear brother and co-worker for more than twenty-years" (Brother Yun with Paul Hattaway, *The Heavenly Man* [Grand Rapids, MI: Monarch Books, 2002]. Yun and Xu spent time in prison together, grew house churches in China together, and watched God perform miracles together. In prison, Brother Xu physically carried Yun around to ensure he was fed and washed after his legs were broken during prison beatings. Xu also greatly encouraged him to continue in his calling to spread the gospel. Lifelong friendship and deep bonds of love develop when people minister together, particularly in adversity.

Love between companions is an essential ingredient before one is willing to sacrifice for a companion. It is also the prerequisite before one can endure persecution with a companion. Love is the primary factor that stops one from entertaining jealousy, pride, and suspicion toward a companion. Without a deep and abiding love for a companion, you only have a friendship: a working relationship, but not companionship.

HANDLING THOSE WHO DESERT OR DISAPPOINT YOU

The first person we see to abandon Paul on his missionary journey was young John Mark (also called Mark), nephew to Paul's colleague Barnabas. When Barnabas suggested taking Mark on their second missionary journey, "Paul did not think it wise to take him, because he had deserted them in Pamphylia and had not continued with them in the work" (Acts 15:37 NIV). Paul was so vehement in his position that a great missionary team was broken up that day. It is interesting that this is the last mention of Barnabas in Acts, and there is no reliable information about his subsequent career or death.

There is no question that John Mark was a disappointment to Paul in the beginning. Many believe Mark's refusal to continue with Paul was not due to fear or being homesick, but to Paul's theological stand that salvation was by grace alone, not observation of Jewish tradition and law. Whatever the reason, Mark was not suitable to continue on the first missionary journey, and Paul had not changed his opinion of him on the second journey. Paul could see that Mark was either not ready for the journey or not up to the challenge that faced them. The establishment and encouragement of churches was too important to Paul to risk adding unnecessary complications with the unpredictable John Mark. However, John Mark reappears in Colossians 4:10, where Paul sends Mark's greetings and endorses him to the Colossian church. In Paul's second letter to Timothy, he wrote, "Get Mark and bring him with you, for he is useful to me for ministry" (4:11). Apparently, not only had Mark become useful to Paul, but he also later proved indispensable to the apostle Peter (1 Peter 5:13).

Probably one of the lowest times in Paul's life was during his trials in Rome. After all the time and energy, prayers and tears spent over so many, no one came to his defense. They all fled in the face of trouble, or at least could not be present with him: "You know that everyone in the province of Asia has deserted me, including Phygelus and Hermogenes" (2 Tim. 1:15 NIV). "At my first answer no one was beside me, but all deserted me. May it not be laid to their charge. But the Lord stood with me and strengthened me" (2 Tim. 4:16–17 MKJV). During these times Paul had to fall back on the one true Companion that had promised never to leave him nor forsake him. The One who had called Paul into ministry was the same One who stood by his side and ministered to him in the darkest hours.

Demas, whom we already mentioned, shared Paul's troubles on his first imprisonment in Rome but did not continue with him in ministry: "Demas, because he loved this world, has deserted me" (2 Tim. 4:9–10 NIV). Demas was certainly considered among his faithful companions (Philem. 1:24, Col. 4:14), but due to his unwillingness to face further hardship and discomfort, he returned to his home in Thessalonica. He left a big hole in the ministry team and in Paul's support network, so Paul called to Timothy and urged him to come quickly upon Demas's departure. We do not hear of Demas again.

Only a few verses later, (2 Tim. 4:14) Paul said of Alexander the metalworker, "[He] did me a great deal of harm" (NIV). Paul's conclusion was "the Lord will repay him for what he has done." He then warned Timothy to be on his guard against him: "You must also beware of him, for he has greatly resisted our words" (v. 15). Of others he said, "Some have rejected [faith and a good conscience] and so have shipwrecked their faith. Among them are Hymenaeus and Alexander, whom I have handed over to Satan to be taught not to blaspheme" (1 Tim. 1:19–20 NIV). Although Alexander cannot be considered a companion to Paul, this passage reveals Paul's attitude toward those who had done him harm or disappointed him and how he left them in God's hands for His judgment. Certainly if people left because of moral failure or outright opposition to him, he felt it was his obligation to warn other believers. But I believe Paul knew much about grace and applied it to his relationships with others liberally.

> **Paul knew much about grace and applied it to his relationships with others liberally.**

I have had to say good-bye to many colleagues over the years. Some of them left when God called them to other ministries, and they departed with my blessing and encouragement. Others left because they could not take the cold weather, the anti-American sentiments among some Canadians, the cultural differences, or simply being away from family back home. They were unable or unwilling to take the pressure and make the sacrifice that pioneer missions requires. Their departures caused a greater stress on me personally until God could find others to replace them.

Paul was never vindictive toward those who abandoned him, nor did he wish them harm. Rather, he was always redemptive in his heart, as he proved with John Mark.

In his letter to the Thessalonian church, Paul warned of those who might not want to listen to or follow his teachings: "If anyone does not obey our word in this epistle, note that person and do not keep company with him, that he may be ashamed. Yet do not count him as an enemy, but admonish him as a brother" (2 Thess. 3:14–15). Here Paul is explicit in how to treat those who err and what sort of relationship believers should have with them. Still, he was full of grace and compassion, not revengeful or harsh. He knew that the goal was to win them as brothers, not drive them away as adversaries.

WHAT DO YOU DO WHEN YOU ARE ALONE?

According to Acts 24:23–27, Paul was imprisoned in Caesarea for more than two years. We have no record of his activities there except for a few visitors who took care of his needs and some conversations Paul had with the governing authorities. During this period in Paul's life, he could only fall back on the promise of his Lord that He would never leave nor forsake him. He had to rely on the presence of the everlasting companion, the Spirit of God, and the periodic visits of friends, possibly Luke among them, and relatives. It would have been a time when Paul rested from missionary travels and reflected on the many places he had seen and lives he had touched. No doubt the many long hours spent alone would have allowed him uninterrupted time in fervent prayer for God to strengthen the faith of others. Some believe that it was during this time that Luke wrote his Gospel.

In Athens, Paul spent some time alone in ministry, reasoned in the synagogue and in the marketplace, and debated with philosophers. Though a few believed, no church was established that we know of. Alone, he continued in his ministry, but clearly his effectiveness was diminished compared to that in other cities where he had preached. Feeling the weight of the need for the gospel to be preached, he sent for Silas and Timothy to join him immediately, but they were not able to join him there. Without companions, there was no one to corroborate his testimony. No one could back up his claims or support his message. There was no one to stand with him in the gospel message, and his hearers, though they found Paul interesting, did not take him very seriously. He then left for Corinth, where he was refreshed by new acquaintances and fellow tent makers Aquila and Priscilla.

When I moved to Saskatchewan in 1970, we were all alone in ministry. No family, no colleagues, no support, and many said we were moving out of the mainstream and going into a place where we would never be heard from again. We faced an entire province where we pastored one of only two churches in our denomination. My heart cried out for someone to help carry the load of ministry and to fulfill the awesome task of planting churches in this vast region. After two years of work, I called a longtime friend and prayer partner from seminary days, Jack Connor, to join me. We had the same heart for missions and the same call to ministry. His coming to work with us was a great encouragement to me personally and to many others who worked with him over the years. To have a companion in ministry made all the difference in those early days, and our effectiveness working together was multiplied.

HOW PAUL DISCIPLED HIS COMPANIONS

I could dedicate an entire book to the discipling methods of Paul, but we can catch a glimpse from the verses below of his focus and aims in discipling others. Paul saw much potential in young Timothy and affirmed him, even though others might look down on his youth. He gave Timothy very clear instructions on how to live out his calling:

> Don't let anyone look down on you because you are young, but set an example for the believers in speech, in life, in love, in faith and in purity. Until I come, devote yourself to the public reading of Scripture, to preaching and to teaching. Do not neglect your gift, which was given you through a prophetic message when the body of elders laid their hands on you. Be diligent in these matters; give yourself wholly to them . . . Watch your life and doctrine closely. Persevere in them, because if you do, you will save both yourself and your hearers. (1 Tim. 4:12–16 NIV)

On several occasions Paul addressed Timothy's timidity and encouraged him not to be ashamed:

- to testify about the Lord (2 Tim. 1:8)

- of Paul as a prisoner (2 Tim. 1:8)

- of suffering for Christ (2 Tim. 1:12)

Paul pleaded with Timothy to stay the course and follow his example and his teachings: "What you heard from me, keep as the pattern of sound teaching, with faith and love in Christ Jesus. Guard the good deposit that was entrusted to you—guard it with the help of the Holy Spirit who lives in us" (2 Tim. 1:13–14 NIV). "Timothy, my son, I give you this instruction in keeping with the prophecies once made about you, so that by following them you may fight the good fight, holding on to faith and a good conscience" (1 Tim. 1:18–19 NIV).

Other verses of instruction (NIV) read:

- "Train yourself to be godly. For physical training is of some value, but godliness has value for all things, holding promise for both the present life and the life to come" (1 Tim. 4:7b–8).

- "But as for you, continue in what you have learned and have become convinced of, because you know those from whom you learned it, and how from infancy you have known the holy Scriptures, which are able to make you wise for salvation through faith in Christ Jesus" (2 Tim. 3:14–15).

- "I give you this charge: Preach the Word; be prepared in season and out of season; correct, rebuke and encourage—with great patience and careful instruction" (2 Tim. 4:1b–2).

To the believers in the church in Thessalonica, Paul wrote,

- "We have confidence in the Lord that you are doing and will continue to do the things we command" (2 Thess. 3:4 NIV).

- "So then, brothers, stand firm and hold to the teachings we passed on to you, whether by word of mouth or by letter" (2 Thess. 2:15 NIV).

- "For you yourselves know how you ought to follow our example. We were not idle when we . . . worked night and day, laboring and toiling so that we would not be a burden to any of you. We did this, not because we do not have the right to such help, but in order to make ourselves a model for you to follow" (2 Thess. 3:7–9 NIV).

Let me just point out that not only did Paul write letters to instruct, encourage, and exhort believers, but he often spent lengthy times with them, leading by example. He stayed a year and a half in Corinth on his first visit, helping to establish a church and ground the believers in their faith, and three months on the second visit. He spent two years in Ephesus. Paul regularly demonstrated his faith as much as he preached about it.

Paul did not keep God's truth for himself but willingly shared it for the encouragement of others, particularly Timothy. He provided young Timothy with both warnings to heed and truth that God had revealed to him. Paul needed to impart spiritual truths to trusted companions, who would faithfully teach it to others. Read the following verses from the New International Version:

- "The Spirit clearly says that in later times some will abandon the faith and follow deceiving spirits and things taught by demons. Such teachings come through hypocritical liars, whose consciences have been seared as with a hot iron . . . If you point these things out to the brothers, you will be a good minister of Christ Jesus, brought up in the truths of the faith and of the good teaching that you have followed" (1 Tim. 4:1–2, 6).

- "But mark this: There will be terrible times in the last days. People will be lovers of themselves, lovers of money, boastful, proud, abusive, disobedient to their parents, ungrateful, unholy, without love, unforgiving, slanderous, without self-control, brutal, not lovers of the good, treacherous, rash, conceited, lovers of pleasure rather than lovers of God—having a form of godliness but denying its power. Have nothing to do with them" (2 Tim. 3:1–5).

- "For the time will come when men will not put up with sound doctrine. Instead, to suit their own desires, they will gather around them a great number of teachers to say what their itching ears want to hear. They will turn their ears away from the truth and turn aside to myths" (2 Tim. 4:3).

Paul had an urgent sense that being a faithful companion to Timothy would be crucial because of his influence on the spiritual lives of many other believers in the churches to whom he ministered. Not only would Timothy be important to the future of the church, but so would those he would teach: "You then, my son, be strong in the grace that is in Christ Jesus. And the things you have heard me say in the presence of many witnesses entrust to reliable men who will also be qualified to teach others" (2 Tim. 2:1–2).

I have spent hundreds of hours with companions in ministry. I traveled those lonely roads into northern Saskatchewan with Len and with Jack, helping them establish mission points and Bible studies. I gave them counsel, support, and encouragement to be successful ministers in their own right. And they in turn did the same for me. We were able to walk together as companions in ministry, and together we rejoiced to see the goodness of God.

GOD USES COMPANIONS TO SHAPE YOU AND YOUR MINISTRY

We were able to better define what our ministry was to be through the companionship of those who partnered with us in Canada. When Jack Conner came to pastor the mission church in Prince Albert, it freed me to focus on other aspects of ministries, such as theological training of new pastors. I had been traveling ninety miles north to Prince Albert twice a week for two years to help establish this new work. Jack helped us discern the will of God and determine what assignments God was giving us.

I recall on one occasion, when Jack and I were praying together, that God revealed to us that He wanted us to begin a theological college to train pastors who could lead all the churches God would begin through our ministry. Jack then spontaneously offered his personal library, his time to teach, and his investment in the lives of young men and women. Jack and I made a covenant that there was nothing either of us would withhold to help each other accomplish what God called us to do. I don't recall one complaining word from Jack, who literally moved up to Canada by faith and continued to live by faith. Many families came to help us in the planting of churches over the years, and many of them, like Jack and Bonna Conner, sacrificed a great deal in doing so.

My son Tom likes to get to the bottom line of an issue quickly in order to make decisions and move on to other issues. But this is not always possible when it comes to problems people face. Tom will readily acknowledge that he comes up short on the scale for showing mercy. He has areas of strength in his character, but mercy is not one of them. God knows this as well, and that is why God brought several deacons in his church whose strengths include mercy. It is no coincidence that when a situation arises that calls for mercy, these particular deacons are nearby! Tom could easily apply justice, exhortation, and truth, but he knows that for the best interests of the body to be served, he needs to let his merciful deacons step up and handle certain situations. Tom has learned mercy from the merciful and compassion from the compassionate, and his character and ability to minister continue to be shaped by those God sends as companions in ministry.

We are all shaped by the people who surround us and by the circumstances in which God places us. It is true that we grow more through challenges and difficulties than at any other time, and it is during these times that we can learn most from our companions. As we lean on their strengths, our weaknesses are improved. As we watch God work through their spiritual gifts, we gain an appreciation for the deliberate differences the Spirit has created us to have.

> **One of the great things about working in ministry is that we can all learn from one another.**

One of the great things about working in ministry is that we can all learn from one another. Tom has learned a great deal from watching the different leadership styles of pastors, laypersons, ministry leaders, and many other people. He also takes pleasure in helping people develop their leadership abilities. The advice he shares with people on conducting meetings, working with a committee, and administrating a ministry has come from watching God's servants who were good at these things. In this way, people's strengths can be used to encourage, shape, and develop strengths in those that follow them.

WHEN COMPANIONS DISAGREE . . .

Paul was the first to admit that he was not perfect. In fact, like all of us, sometimes he could be downright stubborn and argumentative. He didn't always agree with his companions. You will find that in ministry, you will not always agree with your companions. The disagreement between Paul and Barnabas over John Mark (Acts 15:36–41) shows that companions do not always agree. I believe this is an example of what happens when there is a difference in ministry focus. Barnabas delighted in training young ministers, such as Paul, and John Mark was full of potential. Barnabas wisely continued to be a companion to John Mark, to the future benefit of Paul. Paul would learn to be an investor in the lives of others, but he was so focused on the task of church planting that he neglected the immediate priority of people.

To his credit, Paul did not burn bridges in his relationship with young John Mark. When Barnabas had done all he could do in the life of his young nephew, Paul took over and began to invest in Mark's life. It is a testimony to God's faithfulness that He can take our mistakes and turn them into wonderful opportunities to bring Him glory.

. . . And When Companions Move On

At a certain point, we read that Paul's ministry partner changed. He began traveling with Silas, and some of the best stories of Paul's ministry are from this time. From here on, though, Barnabas, the friendly giant in the faith, is not heard of again. We can only guess that there were others God led him to who needed encouraging and strengthening.

When Jack went on to work at the associational level and then the national level in our convention of churches, we still remained good friends, but our relationship was not the same as in the early days. Our ministry foci became different, and we didn't have the opportunities to work together as we had done previously. I believe it is one of God's strategies to send companions who can shape our lives so that God can take each of us off to other assignments in His time. There is a time when a companion's relationship with you may change. Don't become possessive, negative, or vindictive if a companion moves on, but rejoice that God gave him or her to you for the time that you had.

I think in some ways, Paul grew past his companion Barnabas. There is a definite change in the narrative of Acts, which starts by referring to "Barnabas and Saul" (Acts 12:25) and then switches the order to "Paul and Barnabas" (Acts 13:43). It was clear that Paul had become more prominent than his older companion. But there was never any indication of a change in relationship between the two friends. Perhaps the change in narrative reflects how well Barnabas was doing as an encourager to Paul.

> **Don't become possessive, negative, or vindictive if a companion moves on, but rejoice that God gave him or her to you for the time that you had.**

When a lifelong companion dies in a long and fruitful marriage, the remaining spouse can choose either to seek another life companion or shy away from ever experiencing such a loss again. A person might also ask, "Do I ever want to get close to a companion if God is just going to take him [or her] away from me?" Don't prevent God's "sent ones" from affecting you. That is why God has sent them—to affect you! Your plans may not be the same as God's plans for your life, and you will need companions to help interpret God's will in your life and to add abilities and aspects to your ministry that you would otherwise not have. Paul moved on to minister alongside Silas and Timothy, though I am sure he had a special place in his heart for Barnabas.

By the end of Paul's life, he had dozens of people he could claim as dear brothers and sisters in Christ. Whether or not he ever saw them again on this earth did not diminish his affection for them. He knew that he would see them again one day when they stood before their Lord and Savior, Jesus Christ. It was Christ who had called him into ministry, who had spent three years training him, and who was with him at the end. His years of training and his missionary travels prepared him for the end. But though there may have been times when he was physically alone, there were hundreds of friends praying for him around the world: "Finally, brothers, pray for us that the message of the Lord may spread rapidly and be honored, just as it was with you. And pray that we may be delivered from wicked and evil men, for not everyone has faith" (2 Thess. 3:1 NIV).

And in return he prayed often for them: "Remember that for three years I never ceased to warn everyone [of you] night and day with tears" (Acts 20:31); "for I wrote you out of great distress and anguish of heart and with many tears, not to grieve you but to let you know the depth of my love for you" (2 Cor. 2:4 NIV). Paul knew there was a "law of Christ" in companionship, that is, to carry the burdens of those God puts in your life: "Bear one another's burdens, and so fulfill the law of Christ" (Gal. 6:2). Whose burdens do you bear?

STUDY QUESTIONS

1. Paul had an incredible devotion to his companions and to the churches he had started. Read Acts 20:31 and 2 Corinthians 2:4. How do these passages make you feel? When was the last time you shed tears over the welfare of those in whom you were investing your life?

2. How do you see the following quote reflected in your ministry: "His heart's desire was to draw them to Christ in love rather than to drive them by his authority"?

3. In column I below, put the names of two or three people whom you see as either an acquaintance, friend, partner, or companion to you. In column II, place names of those to whom you see yourself as an acquaintance, friend, partner, or companion.

	I	II
Acquaintance		
Friend		
Partner		
Companion		

4. Define the concept of *koinonia* in your own words. To what degree do you see it reflected in your own relationships?

5. Paul seems to have had a definite idea of those spiritual qualities he wanted to build into the lives of those he discipled. Do you have a plan for discipling others? Take a few moments to list five to ten things you believe are essential components of a strong Christian life.

6. Is it possible that you have experienced jealousy because of how God seems to be using another person more than you? Do you notice how difficult it is to rejoice with that person? Can you see how not supporting or encouraging that individual actually hurts you and the kingdom of God?

7. Have you had friends or companions who have deserted you? What is your attitude toward them now? Can you love them and treat them as you would treat Christ?

8. Have you experienced times when you felt completely alone? How did the Lord sustain you in those times? How did you come to know Him more intimately as you allowed Him to meet your needs?

9. What do you do when close friends or colleagues disagree with you? Are you open to the fact that God may have sent them to disagree with you on purpose? Are you redemptive and do you have a spirit of humility when you talk with them?

FOUR

Paul's Major Companions

In sharing the gospel with the Gentiles, none of the eleven original apostles ever went with Paul. Paul spent some time with them in Jerusalem, and even names James, John, and Peter as extending him the hand of fellowship. But none seemed willing to come with him on his journeys. Perhaps the apostles needed to stay in Jerusalem to teach and train those who would be dispersed around the Roman Empire and who would become the core of Paul's churches. (In many places Paul went, he found believers already there, likely the products of the apostles' ministry.)

But God would not have Paul minister alone, for that is not God's way. God placed various people at Paul's side for ministry, companionship, encouragement, and a host of other reasons. Many played significant roles in his life and ministry; others had lesser roles. We will devote this chapter to those whose roles were larger, for these were the ones on whom Paul depended for more than mere companionship. Often they refreshed his heart, encouraged him when he was discouraged and alone, and, on various occasions, risked their own lives for him.

As you read about each major companion that God brought to Paul, ask the Holy Spirit to bring to your mind those He has brought (or is bringing) to your life. Think carefully about the uniqueness of each one. Ask God to evaluate how you have received each one God has sent to you. If no names come to mind, ask God to forgive you for not being alert to receive into your life and ministry His gifts of grace to you in the form of companions that He knows you have needed.

Synergos is a Greek word that is translated "coworker." From this we get our word *synergism*, which means that the sum total of two or more elements working together is greater than their combined efforts could have achieved individually. This is also true of companions, not only because they inspire one another to achieve more than they would have individually, but because the Holy Spirit is at work through them at the same time. God is always able to do far more through His people than they ever could do on their own. The combinations of companions that He puts together are perfectly fitted and joined, as long as Christ remains in the center of their relationship. This is just as true in marriage as it is in ministry.

The following people are those who seem to have had the most investment in Paul's life and ministry. We keep mentioning both *life* and *ministry* because they are so interconnected; one has a direct effect on the other. When companions addressed Paul's personal needs, he was able to minister far more effectively. When they helped him in his ministry, it greatly reduced the strain and stress he felt personally. Read about God's greatest servants and companions to Paul:

PRISCILLA AND AQUILA

Prisca and Aquila, my fellow workers in Christ Jesus, who risked their necks for my life. I am thankful to them, and so are all the churches among the gentiles. Greet also the church in their house. (Rom. 16:3–5 ISV)

Priscilla and Aquila were yokefellows in Christ who had fled Rome under the decree of Claudius because they were Jews (Acts 18:2). According to Paul, they had risked their lives for him (Rom. 16:4). Not only were they workers in God's kingdom, but fellow workers in Paul's trade of tent making. Together they labored side by side, manufacturing tents with their hands and sharing the gospel with their voices. They offered what few others seemed to have, a husband-and-wife team with a strong marriage and a godly home where Paul could relax. In fact, one was never mentioned without the other; they were a couple centered on Christ.

One suspects that Priscilla (also called Prisca) was the more energetic of the two, as she is more often mentioned before her husband. We are not sure when they were converted to Christ, but it may have been under Paul's instruction as he worked alongside them in Corinth. They proved to be fast learners as they accompanied him to Ephesus, where they stayed and tutored Apollos in the knowledge of Christ (Acts 18:26).

They were a stabilizing presence for Paul after traveling so many long roads and staying in so many strange places. It was in their home that a church was birthed in Ephesus. Later, in Rome, their home was once again the site for a new church (Rom. 16:3–5). They helped to stabilize, encourage, and grow several churches in Asia Minor, working with Timothy as their pastor in Ephesus. They were thoroughly steeped in the Old Testament, so Paul did not have to worry about their theology or doctrine. He could leave whole portions of the work in their capable hands without apprehension. They always had a positive word to say about Paul. Their rich heritage in the Scriptures and the stability of their home life were great assets to Paul and to the church. Likewise, the heritage and religious background of a companion is very important and can prove invaluable during times of persecution, instability, confusion, and distress.

> **The heritage and religious background of a companion is very important and can prove invaluable during times of persecution, instability, confusion, and distress.**

TIMOTHY

> But I trust in the Lord Jesus to send Timothy to you shortly, that I also may be encouraged when I know your state. For I have no one like-minded, who will sincerely care for your state. For all seek their own, not the things which are of Christ Jesus. But you know his proven character, that as a son with his father he served with me in the gospel. Therefore I hope to send him at once, as soon as I see how it goes with me. (Phil. 2:19–23)

Timothy is known as Paul's "son in the faith" (1 Tim. 1:2). His name means "honoring God," and he was arguably the most important companion to Paul. Timothy was young, but unlike John Mark, there was no hint of defection in him. He was converted by Paul on his first trip through Lystra (Acts 16; 1 Tim. 1:2; 2 Tim. 3:11). Seven years later, on Paul's second missionary journey, the boy had grown up and was highly recommended to Paul by the church elders as being particularly suitable for missionary work. Paul then took Timothy and circumcised him to remove any impediment to his effectiveness as a missionary (Acts 16:3) to either the Jews or the Gentiles. The fact that he was well grounded in the Scriptures from childhood was a tremendous advantage (2 Tim. 3:15) and proved to be a strong foundation upon which Paul could build (Phil. 2:19–23).

Paul invested more in Timothy's life than any other and could say, "But you have carefully followed my doctrine, manner of life, purpose, faith, longsuffering, love, perseverance, persecutions, afflictions" (2 Tim. 3:10–11). Paul demonstrated great affection for this young apprentice and expressed care for both his spiritual and physical well-being (1 Tim. 5:23).

In return, Timothy did not hide his affections and admiration for his mentor (2 Tim. 1:4). He was so close to Paul that Paul listed him as co-author of six of his letters (2 Corinthians, Philippians, Colossians, 1 and 2 Thessalonians, and Philemon). Timothy was trusted to take Paul's messages and represent his heart to the churches on more than one occasion: "Therefore, when we could no longer endure it, we thought it good to be left in Athens alone, and sent Timothy, our brother and minister of God, and our fellow labourer in the gospel of Christ, to establish you and encourage you concerning your faith" (1 Thess. 3:1–2). Paul also wrote two letters to Timothy personally.

We find Timothy also shared the distinction of being a fellow prisoner with Paul (Heb. 13:23). It was Timothy whom Paul asked to come quickly as Paul neared his last days (2 Tim. 4:9) and had been abandoned by many others. The last recorded words of Paul to Timothy declare his hope to see him one last time if at all possible (2 Tim. 4:21).

BARNABAS

Then Barnabas departed for Tarsus to seek Saul. And when he had found him, he brought him to Antioch. So . . . for a whole year they assembled with the church and taught a great many people. And the disciples were first called Christians in Antioch. (Acts 11:25–26)

As they ministered to the Lord and fasted, the Holy Spirit said, "Now [set apart for] me Barnabas and Saul for the work to which I have called them." (Acts 13:2)

Barnabas was named "Joses" and renamed "son of prophecy" or "encouragement" by his peers because of his character and manner. He was a Levite and a Cypriot by birth. We surmise his first meeting with Paul was in Jerusalem, where he served as a prophet and minister with the apostles. But some speculate that he and Paul could have been educated together in Tarsus, or earlier in Jerusalem. Barnabas befriended Paul and brought him to the apostles (Acts 9:27), establishing a relationship that would continue over many years. Later, he was led of God to search out Paul back in Tarsus and bring him to Antioch, where Paul could hone his preaching skills and be grounded in the ways of Christ. This continued for a whole year in that church before they were set apart by God, affirmed by the elders, anointed, and sent off on the first recorded missionary journey (Acts 13:3).

Barnabas the Levite, godly, generous, and righteous, gave legitimacy to Paul and his message, as he was highly respected in the church in Jerusalem and in Antioch. He helped to orient Paul to kingdom work and people. Barnabas's strength was identifying potential kingdom workers, such as Paul and John Mark, and helping establish them in ministry. He played an extremely important role in setting the foundations of Paul's ministry, introducing him to the apostles and brethren, and supporting him in his call and first missionary journey. God saw Barnabas as the best initial companion to Paul. He was the pacesetter for how Paul would be a companion to others. We are always indebted to those who help establish us in our faith.

We last hear of Barnabas at the Markan dispute (Acts 15:36ff). But even following their disagreement, Paul never spoke a critical word of Barnabas. After their separation, Paul still commended Barnabas to others.

SILVANUS (SILAS)

Now Judas and Silas, themselves being prophets also, exhorted and strengthened the brethren with many words. (Act 15:32)

His name means "wood" and implies that he was a Hellenistic Jew. He and Paul were Roman citizens (Acts 16:37), and Luke described him as a prophet (Acts 15:32). Silas was a delegate from the Jerusalem council, who accompanied Paul and Barnabas to verify the work of God in Antioch (Acts 15:22). Paul must have been quite impressed with Silas and his ministry heart, because he was chosen to join Timothy and him on his second missionary journey to encourage the churches (Acts 15:36). Silas was the next level of companion that Paul needed. He was one who would rejoice in sharing in the suffering for Christ: "who now rejoice in my sufferings on your behalf, and I fill up the things lacking of the afflictions of Christ in my flesh, on behalf of His body, which is the church" (Col. 1:24 MKJV).Silas was incorruptible, grounded in knowledge of the Scriptures, and a well-respected prophet and teacher among the brethren. Paul believed that he was well able to help in confirming the churches (Acts 15:41) in the faith.

If true character is revealed in adversity, then Silas was a gem. Though he was beaten, bloodied, hungry, and unjustly imprisoned (Acts 16:25), he and Paul were praying and singing praises to God in the late hours of night as the other prisoners listened. He embodied Paul's exhortations to rejoice in suffering for the Lord and revealed the contrast between the Christian way of dealing with hardship and the world's way.

Their miraculous release from prison was not the goal of their praise and worship; it was the result. Silas proved a worthy companion to Paul at a time of harsh persecution. He assisted both Paul, in writing the letters to the Thessalonian church, and the apostle Peter (1 Peter 5:12), in delivering his message to believers.

LUKE

"Beloved physician" (Col. 4:14) and "fellow laborer" (Philem. 1:24).

Although he was a physician by trade, Luke was best known as an evangelist. His name is contracted from *Lucanus*, which is a slave name. Luke was likely a freedman practicing a profession not uncommon to slaves. It is probable that he worked in Troas, and was there converted by Paul, to whom he attached himself in ministry. It is telling that Luke wrote more than any other New Testament writer, yet so little is said about him personally. This humble doctor thought more about telling the story of Christ and the acts of the apostles than about getting his own name in history.

Luke was indispensable to Paul during his ministry travels, accompanying him on his first journey and his third, including his voyage to Jerusalem and on to Rome itself (Acts 16:10–17; 20:5–15; 21:1–18; 27:1–28:16). Luke was more than Paul's personal physician; he was truly a companion and the only one to stay with Paul to the bitter end: "Only Luke is with me" (2 Tim. 4:11).

> **This humble doctor thought more about telling the story of Christ and the acts of the apostles than about getting his own name in history.**

Some believe Luke wrote his Gospel and the book of Acts either during Paul's Roman imprisonment or while Paul was in a Caesarean jail. His writings target Gentile believers—the ones whom Paul was called to convert—to strengthen them and encourage them. He was an astute observer of the human condition and had a keen eye for detail. He likely spent time in Jerusalem with James and Peter (and with Mark in Rome) and had ample opportunity to interview eyewitnesses to secure a more accurate account of Christ's life (Luke 1:1–4). His missionary heart and his willingness to suffer with Paul bonded him to Paul as a companion, but his companionship with Paul had a much larger dimension to it than a mere traveling partner. God had in mind for Luke to write both a Gospel and an orderly account of his activity in building and growing the churches.

JOHN MARK

Mark can be very helpful to me, so please find him and bring him with you. (2 Tim. 4:11 CEV)

Some suspect Mark of being an eyewitness to the arrest of Jesus (Mark 14:51–52), though this cannot be proven. He was converted under Peter's guidance (1 Peter 5:13) and grew up among the apostles and church leaders in Jerusalem, many of whom frequented his mother's (Mary) home regularly (Acts 12:12). A relative of Barnabas's, he was a natural choice to accompany Paul and Barnabas on their first missionary journey. Both Paul and Barnabas must have seen much potential in young John Mark as a helper, for he was permitted to join them as an assistant (Acts 13:5).

Few others caused Paul to react so strongly as Mark. Having left Paul and Barnabas in Pamphylia on the first missionary journey, Barnabas decided to give him another chance, but Paul refused (Acts 15:38). The text says Paul had a "sharp disagreement" (v. 39 NIV) with his first traveling companion, so much so that they had to part ways. But, though Mark was the reason for the breakup of Paul and Barnabas, he must have had a change of heart, for it was not long before he became well-known among the brethren for his faithfulness and effectiveness in the work of Christ.

Paul soon became aware of Mark's work and recommended him to the Colossian church (Col. 4:10). Mark quickly became attached to Paul and proved to be the companion that Barnabas knew he could be. Paul referred to Mark as his "fellow laborer" (Philem. 1:24). Even though we never hear of Barnabas again, Mark continued to be a friend to the one who once rejected him. Paul's tender heart allowed Mark to use his gifts and talents right alongside Paul in ministry. Near the end of Paul's ministry, he sent a specific request for Mark to come, because, in Paul's words, "he is profitable to me for the ministry" (2 Tim. 4:11 KJV).

TYCHICUS

Tychicus will tell you all the news about me. He is a dear brother, a faithful minister and a fellow servant in the Lord. (Col. 4:7 NIV)

Tychicus is considered to be one of Paul's primary messengers to the churches and is described by Paul as his "dear brother," "faithful minister," and "fellow servant" of the Lord's. These phrases speak to the character of this companion. It seems that every time Paul mentions Tychicus's name, he is being sent or has been sent somewhere (Titus 3:12, 2 Tim. 4:12) to encourage the saints and to report on what God was doing through Paul.

Many people can be trusted to bring a report, but not so many are able to encourage hearts.

Both the churches in Ephesus (Eph. 6:21–22) and Colosse (Col. 4:7) benefited from the ministry of Tychicus. These churches were dear to Paul's heart, and he would have wanted a trusted emissary who would represent him well and be a blessing to the believers. Tychicus was from Asia, so these churches were also dear to his heart, and he was well-known to them. Too many professing Christians were bringing false messages, seeking personal gain, or trying to harm or confuse churches, but not Tychicus. He was a dear brother and a faithful minister, descriptors most people in ministry would love to have used of them.

We know that Tychicus was a good team player and fellow worker because of both Paul's endorsements and those with whom he is mentioned. Colossians 4:7–9 speaks of Tychicus traveling with another one of Paul's favorite people, Onesimus. It seems that Tychicus had two main aims for visiting churches. One was to bring a report from Paul, and the other was to encourage hearts. Many people can be trusted to bring a report, but not so many are able to encourage hearts. This underscores the character and personality of Tychicus, a little-known companion of Paul's, who played an extremely important role in helping establish and grow churches Paul had begun.

TITUS

I thank God, who put into the heart of Titus the same concern I have for you. For Titus not only welcomed our appeal, but he is coming to you with much enthusiasm and on his own initiative . . . he is my partner and fellow worker among you. (2 Cor. 8:16–17, 23 NIV)

Titus means "honorable." We catch a glimpse of Titus's importance to Paul when Paul writes, "I had no rest in my spirit, because I did not find Titus my brother" (2 Cor. 2:13). Titus was a Greek and therefore a Gentile and likely converted by Paul to Christianity, although he is never mentioned in the book of Acts. He was solid in his character and in his understanding of the Scriptures. He was also trustworthy, as he was entrusted with collecting funds from the churches to bring to Jerusalem. Among his strengths were discernment and exhortation. He was particularly useful in straightening out problems in Corinth after Timothy had failed. He was trusted to bring corrective instructions to the Corinthians, and brought back a report in person (2 Cor. 7:6–7). He was also useful in Ephesus and Crete, where it is said he became the overseer or bishop (Titus 1:5).

Titus was one of the few people to receive a personal letter from Paul, and in it Paul described him as "a true son in our common faith" (Titus 1:4). It appears that Titus was less timid than Timothy and was able to enforce Paul's exhortations in Corinth, where Timothy was not. Second Corinthians 12:18 says, "I begged Titus and sent with him the brother. Did Titus overreach you? Did we not walk in the same spirit? Did we not walk in the same steps?" Second Corinthians 8:16 (MKJV) tells us that Titus had the same heart as Paul for the churches, and was able to minister effectively in Paul's place: "But thanks be to God who puts the same earnest care for you into the heart of Titus." It was a great comfort to Paul to have someone so tightly knit to his own heart that he could be trusted to speak and to act as if it were Paul himself. Titus's name is last mentioned in 2 Timothy 4:10, where an imprisoned Paul reports that he has moved on to Dalmatia.

EPAPHRODITUS

Because for the work of Christ he came close to death, not regarding his life, to supply what was lacking in your service toward me. (Phil. 2:30)

Epaphroditus means "fair" or "graceful." He was not a traveling companion of Paul's, but was one who stayed with and ministered to him during a particularly difficult time. In Philippians 2:25, Paul referred to him as "my brother, fellow worker, and fellow soldier, but your messenger" and minister. Paul was grateful to this brother in Christ who went to Rome specifically to minister to his needs while imprisoned: "Indeed, I have all and abound, I am full, having received from Epaphroditus the things sent from you, a sweet-smelling aroma, an acceptable sacrifice, well pleasing to God" (Phil. 4:18). He was a beloved brother to the church in Philippi also, as is indicated by their concern over his sickness.

Though he was near death, God saved him and spared Paul from further sorrow over the death of such a good friend. It is clear that Paul was deeply touched by the selfless compassion Epaphroditus showed him. We can only assume that when he fell seriously ill, it was Paul who fervently sought God's intervention on his behalf.

Paul appreciated his traveling companions a great deal, but those who left everything to come and minister to him held a very special place in his heart. Paul commended Epaphroditus to the church in Philippi, saying, "Receive him therefore in the Lord with all gladness, and hold such . . . in esteem; because for the work of Christ he came close to death, not regarding his life, to supply what was lacking in your service toward me" (Phil. 2:29–30).

ARISTARCHUS

My fellow prisoner Aristarchus . . . (Col. 4:10)

Aristarchus means "best ruler," and he was a native of Thessalonica. He served as Paul's companion on his third missionary tour, along with Gaius, during which time he was dragged into the theater with Gaius by the mob at Ephesus. He accompanied Paul to Asia and then on to Rome (Acts 19:29; 20:4; 27:2), where he became Paul's "fellow prisoner" (Col. 4:10; Philem. 1:23). Some believe Aristarchus was martyred there in Rome. It takes a special person to face such harsh opposition and come out for more! This fighting spirit was most assuredly an inspiration and motivation to Paul.

After three missionary journeys and facing many, many hardships, Paul would have needed some inspiration from fellow believers. Aristarchus was the man for the job. We know little about what his responsibilities were and nothing of his family, and there are no recorded words from this faithful servant and coworker of Paul's. But as Aaron and Hur held up the hands of Moses to win the battle with Amalek, men such as Aristarchus held up Paul's arms to help him minister faithfully to the very end.

EPAPHRAS

Epaphras, who is one of you, a bondservant of Christ, greets you, always laboring fervently for you in prayers, that you may stand perfect and complete in all the will of God. (Col. 4:12)

Epaphras is a contraction of the name *Epaphroditus*. Some of Paul's deepest tributes are given to Epaphras. He came from Colosse, where he was likely the founder of the church there. He was a leader of the church in Asia and brought reports to Paul in Rome. His work in the church is commendable and seen as foundational to the believers (Col. 1:7–8) and an encouragement to Paul. He was thrown into prison there, where he and Paul could console and encourage one another. Yet even in prison, Epaphras's heart was with those in Colosse. Paul wrote, "Epaphras greets you, he being of you, a servant of Christ, always laboring fervently for you in prayers, that you may stand perfect and complete in all the will of God. For I bear him record that he has a great zeal for you and for those who are in Laodicea and those in Hierapolis" (Col. 4:12–13 MKJV). One of the things Epaphras learned was the ministry of intercession. Paul modeled this for him, and this passage reveals he learned quickly the power of prayer and became a colaborer in prayer with Paul for the churches.

The companions God gave to Paul came from many cities, were from different ethnic backgrounds, spoke various languages, had varieties of talents and a host of different abilities, but they all had one thing in common: the Lord Jesus Christ. Their strength of character and their determination to spread the gospel and strengthen believers bonded them together with a common purpose and a common heart. Any differences they may have had gave way to their desire to bring glory to God through working together in His kingdom.

STUDY QUESTIONS

1. Did God reveal anything to you as you read through the names of these companions? If so, what?

2. Look back over the list and notice how many of these companions risked their lives for Paul.

3. How many different nationalities were represented among these companions? Did you notice that Paul did not look for companions with the same background, nationality, gender, or skin color? For Paul to accomplish his mission, many different people from several diverse backgrounds would need to be employed.

4. Which of the above companions do you think you could use most in your ministry today?

5. Can you identify why God might have chosen these particular companions to be with Paul?

6. Do you know of great husband-and-wife teams who serve as companions to God's servants? Would you and your spouse be willing to be one of those couples?

7. Many of Paul's companions seem to have names that matched their contributions to his life and work. What descriptors would you give to the companions God has brought to your life?

FIVE

PAUL'S LESSER-KNOWN COMPANIONS

IN ALMOST EVERY CITY PAUL WENT, he watched for new God-given companions whom he would train, mentor, and then leave to continue God's work in their cities. God was gracious and gave him companions and fellow workers to help him in the ministry nearly everywhere he went. Look at the different names and places included in Acts 20:4: "And Sopater of Berea accompanied him to Asia—also Aristarchus and Secundus of the Thessalonians, and Gaius of Derbe, and Timothy [Lystra], and Tychicus [Asia] and Trophimus [Ephesus] of Asia." In every place God wants a witness, he places strong, loyal, faithful, hospitality-driven leaders who are usually persons of some influence and are well accepted in the community.

This is just as true for communities, companies, organizations, and industries today. These people, both men and women, became the backbone of Paul's church in their city or community. They were the ones Paul depended on to pass on his teachings and to continue in ministry where he left off. The ones Paul identified as "fellow workers," "faithful servants," "ministers," "fellow laborer" and "faithful friend" comprise a distinguished list of trusted friends, many of whom were the first converts in the city in which Paul visited. These important men and women prayed for Paul, traveled with him, funded his travels, sent others to care for him in prison, suffered alongside him, and fiercely defended him. Without these faithful servants of Christ's to carry on His message of salvation, Paul's efforts would all have been for naught.

As you read about these faithful companions whom God brought to Paul, look carefully to your own life also. Since God has called and assigned you in His kingdom, He has not left you alone. Thank Him for each companion whom He has entrusted to you. Ask God to give freshness to you so that you can be a good steward of His grace.

ONESIMUS

Onesimus, a faithful and beloved brother . . . (Col. 4:9)

[Once] he was useless to you, but now he is useful both to you and to me. (Philem. 1:11 CEV)

Onesimus was a runaway slave who had stolen from his master, Philemon, and sought his fortunes in Rome. Here he tried to be inconspicuous and begin life anew as a free man. Though *Onesimus* means "useful" or "profitable," he was hardly so for his master. In fact, he had cost Philemon a great deal. In Rome, however, Paul led Onesimus to faith in Christ and watched as God began to transform his character from the inside out.

Onesimus had come into contact with Paul earlier when Paul helped establish a church in his home. No doubt Onesimus had great admiration for this respected man of God. Something drew Onesimus to visit Paul; we can only assume it was God's Spirit at work. Paul saw beyond the transgressions of a runaway slave and looked to the heart of a new brother in Christ. He would have done anything to prevent this new believer from facing death because of his actions, and called in a debt owed by Paul's good friend Philemon, Onesimus's master. Paul's appeal to Philemon betrays his affection for his new brother in Christ:

> I appeal to you on behalf of my child Onesimus, whose father I have become during my imprisonment. Once he was useless to you, but now he is very useful both to you and to me. I am sending him, that is, my own heart, back to you. I wanted to keep him with me so that he could serve me in your place during my imprisonment for the gospel. (Philem. 1:10–13 ISV)

Paul was by no means wealthy. In fact he likely had no money at all, but Paul was willing to personally pay whatever debts Onesimus owed to Philemon. I suspect Paul was not concerned that Philemon would take him up on his offer. After all, Paul knew the character and heart of Philemon, as well as the debt of love Philemon owed to him. This being said, it is still remarkable that Paul wrote such an unusual letter. This demonstrates the character of Paul and his devotion to his companions.

PHILEMON

Beloved friend and fellow laborer. (Philem. 1:1)

Philemon was an inhabitant of Colosse and apparently a person of some note among the citizens. He was brought to saving faith in Christ through Paul's ministry (Philem. 1:19) and played a prominent role in the Christian community because of his piety and generosity (vv. 4–7). Paul referred to Philemon as a "dear friend and fellow worker" (v. 1 NIV), indicating that he probably held some position of importance in the church at Colosse, which met in his home. Paul took time to mention Philemon's character and how he was personally refreshed through his efforts: "Your love has given me great . . . encouragement, because you, brother, have refreshed the hearts of the saints" (v. 7). Knowing his nature and godly disposition, it causes one to question why Onesimus would risk losing his life by leaving such a generous master. But we are not given the details, only the happy ending.

> **One of Paul's loveliest and most personal letters was written to plead for the life of a friend.**

The letter Paul wrote to Philemon is intriguing. It was not written to quell some uprising among disputing church members or to correct doctrinal fallacies that had sprung up among them. It was not penned to impart deep spiritual truths or to encourage saints under the oppression of persecution. One of Paul's loveliest and most personal letters was written to plead for the life of a friend. This speaks volumes of the impact Paul's companions had on his life and the degree to which Paul would go to act on their behalf. Such was the kind of companion Paul was to others.

APOLLOS

An eloquent man and mighty in the Scriptures. (Acts 18:24)

We first find Apollos (also known as Apollonius or Apollodorus) coming to Ephesus, where Aquila and Priscilla were living. He demonstrated a keen ability to preach the gospel message and to debate with any who opposed him (Acts 18:28). We have no clear record that Apollos and Paul ever met, though they were geographically very close at various times (19:1), and it appears that Paul may have sent Apollos to encourage believers on occasion (Titus 3:13). Apollos demonstrated the same heart for encouraging and establishing churches that Paul had, though it seems his ministry was centered in the cities of Ephesus and Corinth.

It is clear that Apollos did not feel he was under Paul's authority (1 Cor. 16:12), as he refused to go to Corinth when Paul recommended he do so. However, he was willing to do his part. Apollos was, apparently, a much more eloquent speaker than Paul, but there seems to be no jealousy on Paul's part. Some in Corinth actually preferred Apollos to Paul and had developed rival parties in the church (1 Cor. 3:4–6). But Paul could see the value in what Apollos was doing and saw no reason to control or subjugate Apollos under his ministry.

Acts 19:1 indicates that Paul may have had occasion to build upon the foundations of Apollos's ministry, as he instructed disciples who may have been developed by Apollos but had incomplete knowledge of the gospel. Paul described him as "our brother" and recognized him as a gifted colleague on the same scale as Peter (1 Cor. 4:2–6). He knew that for God's kingdom to move forward, God would use whomever He chose, and the more the better, particularly if they were zealous, confident, and eloquent in their speech.

It would have been nearly overwhelming for both Paul and Apollos to minister in the same city, so God developed many teams of evangelists to carry His message. Apollos emulated Paul's companion strategy by teaming up with Zenas the lawyer (Titus 3:13), a person who would likely complement his character and abilities. Paul spoke of jealousy, conceit, bitterness, and hatred as acts of the flesh that are against the Spirit of God. The kind words Paul spoke toward Apollos show Paul's true humility as a servant of God, and his willingness to share the ministry with others and trust God to care for His people.

ONESIPHORUS

He often refreshed me and was not ashamed of my chains. On the contrary, when he was in Rome, he searched hard for me until he found me . . . You know very well in how many ways he helped me in Ephesus. (2 Tim. 1:16–18 NIV)

Onesiphorus was likely from Ephesus and is named by Paul only twice in the New Testament (2 Tim. 1:16–18; 4:19), but his actions left a tremendous impact on Paul's life. Paul gratefully mentioned him with love as having a noble courage and generosity on his behalf during his trials as a prisoner at Rome. Others had deserted and disappointed him (2 Tim. 4:16), but Onesiphorus remained an encourager and supporter. It is likely that other members of his family were also active Christians (2 Tim. 4:19).

Paul may never have seen or heard from him again, but without the timely help of Onesiphorus, we may never have heard of Paul again either.

This seldom-mentioned fellow with the hard-to-pronounce name left an indelible mark on Paul because of his sacrifice and generous heart in the interest of his imprisoned friend. He was a blessing sent by God at a particularly difficult time in Paul's life. He embodied the words of Christ in Matthew 25:36: "I was naked, and you clothed Me; I was sick, and you visited Me; I was in prison, and you came to Me." Paul may never have seen or heard from him again, but without the timely help of Onesiphorus, we may never have heard of Paul again either.

LYDIA

Lydia, . . . who worshiped God. (Acts 16:14)

Lydia was from Thyatira, where there was a guild of dyers, but was living in Philippi when Paul met her. She had a heart for God and worshiped Him by the river, away from the noise of the city. It was there that she met Paul, Silas, and Luke and listened to their message to her from God. God opened her heart to understand and to accept the message of His servants (Acts 16:14), and she became Paul's first European convert to the gospel of Christ. Before, she had come regularly to the river to worship God; now she was baptized in the same river as a follower of Christ. Her conversion was so effective that she led her entire household to faith in Christ. Some believe it was Lydia who took the gospel to Thyatira, where God had prevented Paul from going.

Lydia must have been a woman not only of substantial wealth, but also of considerable influence, for she was able to "constrain" Paul and his companions to come to her house to stay (Acts 16:15 KJV). Here Paul followed instructions Christ gave to His disciples in Matthew 10:11–13: "Now whatever city or town you enter, inquire who in it is worthy, and stay there till you go out. And when you go into a household, greet it. If the household is worthy, let your peace come upon it. But if it is not worthy, let your peace return to you."

Her home became the center of the church activity for Paul whenever he stayed in Philippi. In fact, it was to her home that Paul and Silas went after they were miraculously freed from prison (Acts 16:40). She was more than likely the source of the funding sent with Epaphroditus to minister to Paul's needs in prison (Phil. 4:18). It would not be surprising if Lydia served as a benefactor or patron for Paul's travels.

PHOEBE

I commend to you Phoebe our sister, who is a servant of the church in Cenchrea. (Rom. 16:1)

Phoebe comes from Cenchrea, the eastern port of Corinth. This was the place where Paul had his head shorn to complete a vow he had made (Acts 18:18). The term *servant* here means "deaconess," and Paul mentioned that she had been a supporter of many people, including himself. Phoebe was most likely traveling to Rome and would have been the perfect emissary to the church there. Paul asked those receiving the letter to accord her all the rights and privileges that should be given to a true saint and fellow worker in the gospel.

Perhaps it is noteworthy that Phoebe is at the top of the list of more than thirty people Paul listed in his letter to the Roman church (16:1). I am amazed that, after all the travels of Paul and the many people he ministered to, he could remember not only the names, but cite specific details of so many, such as Epenetus, his first convert in Asia, and Rufus's mother, who acted as a mother to him as well. Three in the list (Andronicus, Junias, and Herodion) Paul described as his relatives. The inclusion of such a list is again a testimony of Paul's heart for people and how valuable their friendships were to him.

This list of lesser-known companions cannot be exhaustive, because there were so many who assisted Paul in so many different ways, serving him as friends, companions, colleagues, coworkers, fellow prisoners, fellow ministers, supporters, encouragers, underwriters, and much more. After reading these last two chapters, you can really get a sense of just how many people were involved in spreading the gospel with Paul.

> **On several occasions all Paul could do was write a letter. He could not go personally to check on his beloved churches, but he could send one whom God had brought him as a companion.**

A cursory glance through the book of Acts might give one the initial impression that Paul was the invincible, unflappable missionary who trudged across Asia Minor with or without companions to share Christ with the Gentiles, stopping from time to time to write half of the New Testament and provide us with a manual on church planting. This just isn't so. Paul had an assignment from God, but it was one that could only be completed in concert with hundreds of other believers who each carried his load and did what God enabled him to do to plant and grow churches.

On several occasions all Paul could do was write a letter. He could not go personally to check on his beloved churches, but he could send one whom God had brought him as a companion. I wonder if God allowed Paul so many prison experiences so that he was compelled to depend on others as he did. We can only speculate. But truly, Paul was not responsible for planting churches and spreading the gospel; Christ was. Paul was only one part of an elaborate plan to bring the good news to the world.

PETER

So when James, Peter, and John (who were reputed to be leaders) recognized the grace that had been given me, they gave Barnabas and me the right hand of fellowship, agreeing that we should go to the gentiles and they to the circumcised. (Gal. 2:9 ISV)

Galatians 1:18 tells us that Paul stayed with Peter fifteen days in Jerusalem after his three years of learning from Christ in Arabia. It is in Jerusalem that Peter maintained his base of operation. Peter is never listed as having traveled with Paul or supporting the church-planting effort. In fact, Paul had to rebuke Peter in Antioch because of his stand on Gentile converts: "Now when Peter had come to Antioch, I [opposed] him to his face, because he was to be blamed" (Gal. 2:11). However, Peter did endorse Paul on several occasions and recognized the God-given authority with which Paul spoke: "Our beloved brother Paul also has written to you according to the wisdom given to him as also in all his letters, speaking in them of these things; in which are some things hard to be understood, which the unlearned and unstable pervert, as also they do the rest of the Scriptures, to their own destruction" (2 Peter 3:15–16 ASV).

Paul recognized that he and Peter had different calls on their lives, but the same Lord. "But on the contrary, seeing that I have been entrusted with the gospel of the uncircumcision, as Peter to the circumcision; for He working in Peter to the apostleship of the circumcision also worked in me to the nations" (Gal. 2:7–8 MKJV). They were on the same team with different positions to play, and they could rejoice together in the victories. It was Paul who helped organize a love offering for the Jerusalem church, collected among "his" churches. Paul recognized the debt he and the rest of the world owed to the original disciples and to their memory of Christ and His teachings.

ANANIAS

> Ananias, a devout man according to the law, having a good testimony with all the Jews who dwelt there, came to me. (Acts 22:11)

The one who helps us come to Christ often sets the stage for the rest of our Christian life. Paul described Ananias as being a "devout man," immersed in the Scriptures, whose reputation was good even among the Jews. He was selected by God to bring Paul to the light both physically and spiritually. Tradition has it that Ananias was the leader in the Damascus church and was likely Saul's target as he traveled to Damascus to imprison Christians. Saul (Paul) had in mind to arrest Ananias, throw him in prison, and destroy what was left of the Damascus church.

What strikes me is that Ananias risked his life for Paul. The word from God was so clear to him that he had no choice but to obey and present himself to the one bent on eradicating him. With fear and trepidation, Ananias's first words to Paul were "Brother Saul . . . the Lord . . . Jesus has sent me" (Acts 9:17 NIV). These would have been comforting words to a troubled and confused Saul, who was desperate for guidance and for Christian love at this point. Ananias helped the man once filled with hate become filled with the Spirit of God. He took Saul, covered in the guilt of Stephen's death, and baptized him, cleansing his soul from sin. Then he humbly taught him about the Christ he had been persecuting and watched one of the most amazing and radical transformations in a person's character ever recorded in Scripture. Paul went from hauling Christians to prison to preaching Christ in the synagogues in a matter of days. But it was Ananias, this wise disciple of Christ's, who held his hand through the transformation process and steadied this wobbly newborn Christian until he could walk on his own feet. Paul must have had a special place in his heart for Ananias and the believers in Damascus, for they were his first brothers and sisters in Christ as he entered the family of God.

Paul went from hauling Christians to prison to preaching Christ in the synagogues in a matter of days.

I look back on the extensive church planting God allowed my companions and me to do in Saskatchewan. It was truly an experience of seeing God at work, for in each town or village or city, God had already strategically placed believers who would help us start the church in their location. Many of these good folk have become longtime friends to us even to this day. Always be alert to those whom God gives you at the beginning of His assignments; they can certainly become lifelong companions and close friends over the years.

STUDY QUESTIONS

1. At the beginning of this book, we stated there were no second fiddles in God's kingdom, as all parts work together to make an incredible symphonic sound. Among the lesser-known companions of Paul, do you notice that even one act of kindness or cooperation with Paul was important to the overall effort?

2. The reason we know of these companions is because of their relationship to Paul. But there is every possibility that they were ministers in their own right, serving God where He placed them. Each of them may have made an incredible impact on his or her own community or city, but Luke does not record it, because that was not his purpose for writing. Will you be content to be faithful to what God calls you to but not get the recognition others receive?

3. Ananias was given one of the most difficult tasks a believer could have been given. He was asked to present himself to the person who had come to arrest and imprison him. His obedience reveals the level of trust Ananias had in God. Yes, he questioned God's instructions, but still he obeyed. I shudder to think what could have happened to the spread of the gospel had he not obeyed. Do you think you are ready for God to entrust a very sensitive and important task to you? What is the likelihood of your immediately obeying rather than putting it off after arguing with God? What might the consequences of your disobedience be?

4. Women sometimes do not receive the recognition they deserve for the important ministry they perform in God's kingdom. When Paul was miraculously released from prison, it was to Lydia's home that he went. Women provide a very special component to companionship and are often more compassionate, gracious, and merciful than men. What impact have godly women had on your Christian life over the years?

5. Did you notice this list includes business owners and slaves, men and women, lawyers and laborers? Every person has a role to play as a companion in God's kingdom. No one is exempt from being an encourager or a fellow worker in God's plan. Do not feel that you are not worthy, educated, or popular enough to be a companion or to have companions. There is a role and an assignment for every believer. Have you found God's role and assignment for you?

6. Ananias had the privilege of opening Paul's eyes to a whole new way of life. Wouldn't it be great if you were the one to "discover" the next servant of God through whom God would do incredible things? Ananias may not have lived to see all that God was able to do through Paul, but he was there at the beginning, helping Paul get on his feet as a new Christian. The lives we invest in today will be the leaders tomorrow. In whom are *you* investing your life at this moment?

7. Paul is known for his vast letter writing. Many of these letters were sent as encouragement to companions. Is your life noted for your letters of encouragement to others?

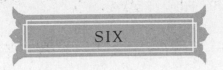

SIX

HONORING THE COMPANIONS GOD SENDS YOU

A GOOD STARTING PLACE for identifying God-sent companions is a study of the lives of both Christ and the apostle Paul. Companions play an awesome role in the life of every servant. This is clearly seen in the mind and heart of both Jesus and the Father. Therefore it is crucial that we recognize who God is sending to us, and when. Jesus knew who God had granted to Him and why. He said to His Father,

> I have manifested Your Name to the men whom You have given me out of the world. They were Yours, You gave them to Me, and they have kept Your Word. Now they have known that all things which You have given Me are from You. For I have given to them the words which You have given Me; and they have received them, and have known surely that I came forth from You; and they have believed that You sent Me. (John 17:6–8)

God sent His Son as a companion (helper) to the twelve disciples, and as Christ dwells in every believer, His presence will be evident in those God sends to you (Gal. 2:20). Our primary verse for this book comes from John's Gospel, where Jesus said, "How you receive the one I send you, you receive me" (13:20).

God may not give you a task like He gave to Paul, but the principle of companionship in the kingdom of God remains the same. It is important to be able to recognize when God is sending you a companion or providing you with a dear friend, colleague, or coworker to help you along the way.

EXPECT GOD-SENT COMPANIONS

The New Testament indicates that Christ purposed for His followers to be a royal priesthood and a kingdom people with a common purpose and a common Lord. The body of Christ is comprised of interconnected and interdependent units (churches) that function within the reality of a larger kingdom. In this day there is a proliferation of independent, unaccountable, self-centered ministries, organizations, and kingdom efforts who will not act in concert with the body of Christ as seen in the local church. In fact, many of them actually compete with the local church, draining its resources both in people and finances to fund their own visions.

God expects His people to work with one another in unity and harmony and will give them one heart and one mind to serve Him together. God never intended His people to compete with each other in His kingdom, but to complement one another in their work. When ministries, organizations, and churches focus on what God has asked them to do, they will not overlap and compete with one another; rather, they will each play a specific role, joined together by Christ, to fulfill His purposes. Too many people and organizations try to be all the body parts when God has only assigned them to be a *specific* body part. They are not able to do everything well because that was not how they were designed from the start.

> God never intended His people to compete with each other in His kingdom, but to complement one another in their work.

You are naturally incomplete as a body part and need those God sends to add what is lacking to ensure your successful obedience. God places at your side those who will affirm His call on your life and the assignment He has given to you. The skills, abilities, and insights of companions will be invaluable to you as you work together toward the completion of God's assignments.

My son Tom has now served in five different churches since God called him into His service. He has served as minister of music/religious education/youth, associate pastor of *everything*, and senior pastor over the years. In each location, he made a habit of seeking out kindred spirits in ministry as well as someone who would walk with him as a companion in ministry. Sometimes the companion was the pastor of the church, as when he served with his older brother, Richard. Other times the companion was an associate pastor in another church or denomination. In one church it was Jim, a denominational worker who called Tom every week to check in on him and to meet him for coffee to see how his ministry was going. Tom works best in a team setting, and because he knows his own weaknesses, he seeks out the wisdom, counsel, and encouragement that companions have to share with him.

Personally, I have never actively pursued companions for my ministry, though I have often tried to be a companion to many people in ministry in order to encourage them in what God has called them to do. I have also agreed with God when He has sent companions to me, because it was all too clear that the assignment He gave me was beyond my abilities, and others were needed to walk with me. God also knew what Paul would face in ministry and the kind of suffering he would endure. In fact, He foretold it. Perhaps this is why Luke, as a lifelong companion, was so valuable to Paul. He needed a doctor to heal the physical wounds of his suffering. It is why God prepared a Tychicus and Apollos to go when Paul could not. It is why young Timothy was called out to walk with Paul and learn from him, so that when Paul's life came to an end, there would be others to carry on.

It would be wise for us to see the gifts and skills of those God sends us as indicators of what we might encounter in the days ahead. I still marvel that God sent a chiropractor to me, who offered to serve me in any capacity that was needed. Because of a particular physical condition, a chiropractor is the professional I most often visit. God knew ahead of time what I would need in order to complete the assignments He gave me. The staggering number of airplane flights, different beds, and long distances I walk carrying suitcases and briefcases have taken their toll on my neck and back. You can imagine how refreshed I am by the timely kindness of a chiropractor.

I have to admit that there have been times in the past when I was not as sensitive to God's prompting and did not pursue certain people who would have been great companions. I thought I knew best, but I realize now that this was to my loss and probably cost me in some way in ministry. I likely did not achieve the results in ministry that God had wanted because I did not accept the companions He was trying to give me. I believe the Holy Spirit guides companions together. Whether the leader identifies the companion or the companion is drawn to a leader, it is still evidence of the Spirit at work in the hearts of His people.

> **The Holy Spirit guides companions together. Whether the leader identifies the companion or the companion is drawn to a leader, it is still evidence of the Spirit at work in the hearts of His people.**

God knew what Paul would need on his missionary journeys. He laid it on the hearts of various people to undergird Paul's ministry and support him in his travels. Men, women, leaders, servants, masters, slaves, rich, and poor were all called by God to share in the work of ministry. Philippians 4:3 says, "I urge you also, true companion, help these women who labored with me in the gospel, with Clement also, and the rest of

my fellow workers, whose names are in the Book of Life." The picture here is that of oxen yoked together, pulling the load with all their strength and working together for good. You can read through a list of nearly thirty names in Romans 16 of those whom Paul saw as fellow workers in the kingdom of God.

GOD MATCHES THOSE HE SENDS WITH THE ASSIGNMENTS HE GIVES

And Sopater of Berea accompanied him to Asia—also Aristarchus and Secundus of the Thessalonians, and Gaius of Derbe, and Timothy, and Tychicus and Trophimus of Asia. (Acts 20:4)

Did you notice the variety of names and places you just read? These were men with a diversity of backgrounds and skills that accompanied Paul for specific reasons. Paul needed a special companion with whom he could serve time in prison. He needed a particular type of companion that he could trust to stay with various churches to help them grow and be established. He needed a specific companion to help heal the many wounds inflicted upon him and guide him through the times of sickness he encountered. He needed companions who were able to teach and preach and debate in the many cities where he proclaimed the gospel. And, I believe, he needed companions just to sit with him during times of loneliness.

As you pray asking God how you are to go about accomplishing your assignment, become sensitive to those He may place in your path or bring to mind from your past. When we were beginning a new component to our current ministry, we received a phone call from some dear friends. They are probably the friends we have known the longest; in fact, they were in our wedding party. Clayton and Lois had been retired for a few years and desired to serve the Lord full-time with their remaining years.

They asked if it would be all right with us if they sold their home and moved to our city to help us in whatever God was calling us to do. Their skills, time, insights, and friendship have been invaluable to us, and their servant hearts are a testimony to their deep and abiding love for God.

Others, such as Bob Dixon and Don Gibson, have reoriented their lives to be fellow workers with me in ministry. None of these had a personal agenda or sought a relationship to further their own ministries or visions. Rather, it was God who put us together because of a common heart and a common vision to make Him known.

I remember two incredible spiritual companions God granted to me in one of the most demanding times in my ministry. Jack Conner and Len Koster had all the qualities of good companions. When God gave us one mind and heart and soul to train and equip those God was calling to serve Him, God guided us to start a theological college in our church. We just called it the Christian Training Centre (later the Canadian Baptist Theological College). We needed a library in which the students could learn and study. Spontaneously, all three of us knew we were to put our personal libraries together (distinguishing our books with colored dots) to make what God had given us available to the students in the school. We knew the books were God's, so we released them to God and those He was calling. This library was available for ten years, and other books were added. None of us saw it as sacrifice, but rather as obedient stewardship. Here was a specific sign of true companions, each of us led by the Spirit, agreeing together, and God bringing Himself the glory.

THE HOLY SPIRIT WILL AFFIRM THE COMPANIONSHIP

Prayer needs to play a significant role in recognizing the companions God sends: "While they were worshiping the Lord and fasting, the Holy Spirit said, 'Set apart for me Barnabas and Saul for the work to which I have called them'" (Acts 13:2 NIV). This is a key verse regarding companionship. It is the Holy Spirit who chooses His servants and matches people in their tasks.

Acts 8 shows a new convert following after Philip and Peter. Simon was astonished at the power God exhibited through these two men. He was an avid follower of Philip's, but it became clear that Simon's heart was not right when he sought to buy the Spirit's power. Many potential followers of Jesus came seeking a position with Him among His disciples, but Jesus refused them because their hearts were divided or they were not truly committed (Luke 9:57–62). God's Spirit will affirm a person's companionship to you and your companionship to them. Both must sense the Spirit's leading, or it is not of God.

Over the years, several people have told me that God has called them to come and work with me in ministry. Some have told me that God wanted my ministry to hire them as paid employees. Others have casually said their lives were available to do whatever they could to help me. But God's Spirit has either warned me not to pursue them or has revealed to me that their character, motives, or life situations were such that they would do far more harm to me in ministry than good. Not everything is always as it seems, and it is imperative that you have God's clear guidance and divine wisdom before allowing people to join with you in ministry.

There may be times in ministry when you come to the realization that your companions no longer have your best interests in mind. There may be occasions when you must release those working with you or separate yourself from them because they have developed a critical spirit or fallen into immorality. Sometimes it may become clear that their hearts have shifted to other things, away from the common vision and ministry you once shared.

Of course, there are also times when you release companions because the Spirit has other plans for them. God may be asking them to follow

Him into new ministries and adventures. At these times I have rejoiced with my companions as they followed God to their next assignment and given them my blessing and encouragement. But any time a companion is released from working with you, regardless of the circumstances, it needs to be bathed in prayer.

Something we taught our children about relationships applies also to identifying companions. We encouraged our five children to look for mates that build them up and bring out the best in them rather than ones who constantly drag them down, distract them from doing God's will, or are so needy that they are not able to pursue the life direction God gave them. A person who holds you back from your ministry is not one who is walking beside you. The rule of synergy is that you are supposed to accomplish more together than your combined individual output could produce. Sometimes you find that people so distract you or complicate things that you are actually producing only half of what you would have normally done without them present!

A person who holds you back from your ministry is not one who is walking beside you. The rule of synergy is that you are supposed to accomplish more together than your combined individual output could produce.

During the twelve years of ministry at Faith Baptist Church in Saskatoon, Saskatchewan, Canada, we watched God do some incredible things. Dozens of churches were planted, student ministry thrived, a theological college was established, and our church was having a significant influence in the city and across the province. Then it was time for me to move to my next assignment in ministry. Under the new pastor the Bible college was deincorporated, student workers were encouraged to leave, and church planting was no longer a priority. Eventually the pastor left the church. I had left it to the church to choose their next pastor, as is customary, but I now realize that Paul's strategy of building and discipling leaders *within* the church to replace him holds great merit.

It is imperative for companions to have one heart, mind, and soul as they work together. If there are constant bickering, compromising, and negotiating when deciding where God is leading, then there is a problem. If, however, there is a heart's desire to discern God's direction together and each one builds on the other's understanding, great things can happen. A companion is one who understands your ministry/call and affirms it to you. Such a person does not have his or her own agenda to fulfill through you, but rather a heart to see you succeed in all that God has set before you to do.

It is impossible to talk about companionship without mentioning David and Prince Jonathan: "Now when he had finished speaking to Saul, the soul of Jonathan was knit to the soul of David, and Jonathan loved him as his own soul . . . Then Jonathan and David made a covenant, because he loved him as his own soul" (1 Sam. 18:1, 3). The phrase *knit to the soul* is very interesting. It means "sameness of mind" as if there were one soul and two bodies. Here is an example of a friend being like another self. God knew how important this friendship would be to the future of His people: Christ would come from the seed of David, and were it not for Jonathan's bond of companionship, David would have been destroyed by his father, King Saul. The bond between the two friends saved David's life and secured the future salvation of the world. There is a lesson to be learned here. Never underestimate the value of a companion; it could mean your life.

> **Never underestimate the value of a companion; it could mean your life.**

HOW TO TREAT COMPANIONS

Companionship is truly a matter of stewardship. Whatever God gives us, including companions, He is entrusting into our care and expecting us to use for His glory. How we treat our companions will be noticed by the One who sends them: "Obey your leaders and submit to them, for they keep watch over your souls as those who will give an account, so that they can do this with joy and not with grief, for that would be unprofitable for you" (Heb. 13:17 HCSB). We should love our companions, care for them, protect them, and help them to grow in the grace of Christ as best we can. We are to pray for them, encourage them, inspire them, and challenge them to be what God wants them to be. We are to lead them by example, love them as brothers or sisters in Christ, and serve them as Christ served His disciples.

Paul offered us an example of how to be transparent before our companions in order to properly develop their ministry skills. To Timothy, Paul wrote, "You, however, know all about my teaching, my way of life, my purpose, faith, patience, love, endurance, persecutions, sufferings—what kinds of things happened to me in Antioch, Iconium and Lystra, the persecutions I endured" (2 Tim. 3:10–11 NIV). Can your companions say that of you? They are certainly watching you to see if you do what you say, if your words match your actions, and if you believe what you preach or teach. But more, Paul deliberately gave Timothy the opportunity to be with him on many occasions and in many situations so that he could see that Paul was the real thing.

One verse that may send shivers down the back of every leader comes from Paul's letter to the Ephesians: "submitting to one another in the fear of God" (5:21). If you can think of even one occasion when you would not be willing to submit to your companion (associate, colleague, coworker, wife, etc.), then you are not ready to have companions, for if God cannot get your attention and bring you a word of truth through your companion, there is no sense in sending them to you! Yes, God can speak truth through those He sends you. Be quick to submit to the message God is speaking through them or your ministry could be jeopardized. Remember, they are accountable to God first for their obedience to Him and must speak as He commands them to speak.

It has grieved me to see pastors who demand the unquestioning submission and blind loyalty of all their staff rather than seeing them as companions and coworkers sent by Christ for a common purpose in His kingdom. They do not realize how offensive their actions are to God. For how they have been treating their staff is how they have been treating His Son! "Truly, truly I tell you, the one who receives whomever I send receives me" (John 13:20 ISV). Would we have the audacity to demand unquestioning loyalty from Jesus? Would we fire Jesus because He did not blindly follow our plans for His church?

Some pastors do not feel they are accountable to deacons, boards, or even the church that called them to shepherd them. They see their staff and church leadership not as companions, but as personal servants or slaves to do their bidding and to build their ministry. Such pastors have their own kingdoms in mind rather than the kingdom of God. It would be difficult for such pastors to say, as did Paul, "For we do not preach ourselves, but Christ Jesus the Lord, and ourselves your bondservants for Jesus' sake" (2 Cor. 4:5). The pastor is not to subjugate his staff, but honor them, listen to them, and serve them as he would serve Christ. He is to walk with them, function with them, and love and cherish them as gifts from God.

Tom learned a great deal about servanthood and being in a supportive role in the various churches in which he served prior to becoming a senior pastor himself. There is no better way to learn how to treat staff than to be one! With most of the pastors, Tom sensed oneness of heart, and it was a joy to work with them. He learned from them and his abilities complemented theirs.

With others, however, he felt his opinion was not valued (much less asked for), and the other staff members were all doing their own thing, with little concern or interaction with the others. Here, ministry was not a joy, nor were the staff relationships pleasing to God. God was not able to bring the staff together because their hearts were not "knit together." They did not feel any sense of being "yokefellows" in ministry. The staff did not socialize together or feel any obligation toward one another's families. This was not companionship in ministry; it was simply people working in the same office.

Unquestioning loyalty to a *pastor* is not a biblical principle; unquestioning loyalty to Christ is. Mutual submission, esteeming others more highly than yourself, servant leadership, and being willing to put your life on the line for your brother or sister *are* biblical principles. For a leader to be upset because his staff questions his decisions (not publicly, but privately) for clarification or accuracy discounts everything God has placed in companions to help sharpen the leader. Companions see things the leader does not. That is why God has brought them. They are not sent primarily to help the *pastor* be successful, but to help *everyone* be successful, including the pastor, as they work together.

> **Unquestioning loyalty to a *pastor* is not a biblical principle; unquestioning loyalty to Christ is.**

Having served as a pastor for twenty-five years and having worked with a good number of staff, I conclude that there does need to be a *leader* who leads. But Christ has *never* relinquished His role as Head of His church to the local pastor. The pastor does play a significant part in the body of Christ as a spiritual leader, discipler, role model, minister, and exhorter, but he still remains only one of many who comprise the body (Rom. 12:4–5; 1 Cor. 12:12).

Have you ever said to God, "I just want to know Jesus more"? I have heard many ministry leaders pray this way. Well, how did you treat the last person He sent you? Christ may want to send someone to you, and if you do not receive that person as you would receive Christ, you have snubbed Christ's efforts to impact your life.

Many, many marriages would be saved if John 13:20 was implemented in the life of each spouse. How you treat your spouse is how you treat Christ. Do not ask God to bless or guide you while you mistreat your wife or husband. How can you expect God to bless you when you are harassing, belittling, criticizing, and demeaning His Son in your spouse? There is no question in my mind that many pastors have failed miserably in ministry because of how they have treated their staff, colleagues, and spouses. First Peter 3:7 tells us that our prayers will be hindered if we mistreat our spouses. Try to run a ministry while God refuses to listen to your prayers; you will find little success. God refuses to bless some people's ministries because they have failed to treat their companions with love, respect, and honor. A wonderful summary truth to guide us comes from 1 John 3:16: "By this we know love, because He laid down His life for us. And we also ought to lay down our lives for the brethren."

INVESTING IN YOUR COMPANION'S LIFE AND THE LIVES OF HIS FAMILY MEMBERS

Now I urge you, brothers—for you know that the members of the family of Stephanas were the first converts in Achaia, and that they have devoted themselves to serving the saints—to submit yourselves to people like these and to anyone else who shares their labor and hard work. (1 Cor. 16:15–16 ISV)

Paul not only invested his life in his companions, but also encouraged and supported their families as well. The sad reality is that the opposite is far too often true: Leaders frequently ignore a companion's family and the companion's own obligation to that family. The family then actually feels deep resentment and disdain toward the leader whom their family member serves as companion. An associate pastor's wife once commented to me that, incredibly, after two years, her pastor's wife still didn't know her name How tragic that people who have given their lives to ministry do not take any interest in one another's personal life, including one's children. The children of your associates, your companions, your fellow workers, should be able to love and respect you so that when the demands of ministry occasionally take their parents from them, you are not to be blamed and personally held responsible. They should also feel a level of kinship with you.

We often had companions in ministry in our home, particularly for Sunday lunch. My children would talk with them, eat with them, and joke with them. Each one of our ministry coworkers made an impact on our children, and many would later become encouragers to our children as they grew up and became involved in ministry themselves. Our children came to recognize the importance of companions to us and learned to love and appreciate our coworkers. They also developed an appreciation for God's people that I believe may not have happened had they not had such personal contact with them in our home. Our children have now each found ways to be companions to others in ministry and have a deep appreciation for the companions God brings to them in ministry.

Despite the demanding travel and workload, Paul devoted a great deal of time and energy, not only to the lives of those God sent to him, but to *every* person who would listen to him:

> To them God willed to make known what are the riches of the glory of
> this mystery among the Gentiles: which is Christ in you, the hope of
> glory. Him we preach, warning every man and teaching every man in all
> wisdom, that we may present every man perfect in Christ Jesus. To this

end I also labor, striving according to His working which works in me mightily. (Col. 1:27–29)

This verse describes Paul's hard work in terms of competing with an adversary, contending for a prize, and struggling with great effort. He was wearied, toiling night and day, praying constantly on behalf of those to whom he ministered. When you look at your companions, coworkers, and fellow ministers, do you see yourself expending energy and time to present them perfect in Christ Jesus? Can you say as Paul, "I labor . . . until Christ is formed in you" (Gal. 4:19)?

Two of Paul's letters were written to disciple, train, and encourage Timothy. The letter to Titus is full of instructions on how to straighten out an erring church in Crete in order to bring glory to Christ. Titus was not left on his own to manage a difficult situation. Paul gave very specific instructions on how a church should behave and live to demonstrate a strong witness to the great salvation they have in Christ. He wanted his companions to find every success possible as they followed his example, practiced his teachings, and pursued God's will for their lives.

We have watched many trying to work in pioneer mission fields, such as Canada, become shipwrecked on the rocks of discouragement. So much of this could have been avoided if they had been working together with others, mutually encouraging and supporting one another. Too often the family of the worker is scarred because of ministry failure and may even leave the church or ministry altogether. It is so incredibly important to ensure that systems are set in place to hold up, hearten, and refresh those in ministry to prevent possible burnout and discouragement. Had Paul not had dear friends to seek him out and come alongside him, the light that was dimming in his eyes in prison might have gone out altogether.

Arthur and Marion Clark were older members of our congregation in Canada. He was a retired accountant from England, and she was a faithful prayer warrior. Together they volunteered to use their retirement for God's kingdom and went to start a church in a small ethnic community in Saskatchewan. They served faithfully for several years trying to lead people to Christ and to start a Bible study. But the small community was tightly controlled by the traditional ethnic religions and refused any cooperation with Arthur and Marion. Though a few adults and several children were brought to Christ, none felt the freedom to commit to starting a church. They came home dejected, frustrated, and feeling very much like failures in ministry. They desperately needed encouragement. They had been obedient to God's call on their lives and served faithfully to the best of their ability. Our church wrapped our arms around them and loved them. They became so special to our church, and were great encouragers, particularly to my own children.

At the time I had no idea what impact my act of love had on Arthur and Marion's family. But I later found out that their daughter and son-in-law entered the ministry partly because of how we walked with her father and mother. I also had the opportunity to meet one of their grand-children, who thanked me and showed me a picture of his grandparents and mentioned to me the wonderful stories they had told of their time in our church. We never know the effect our companionship will have on future generations.

AFFIRMING COMPANIONS

The LORD God gives me the right words to encourage the weary.
(Isa. 50:4 CEV)

Moses did not train Joshua to be a soldier or warrior but gave him opportunities to grow into those roles. Paul often gave his companions assignments, sending them to carry out a variety of tasks, not all of which were pleasant. Still, these companions learned and grew through them (1 Tim. 1:3–4). Dealing with division and strife among believers is very taxing work. Several of Paul's companions were his trusted emissaries to troubled churches. But Paul provided them with what they needed to get the job done, and God worked through them to accomplish the rest. For without God's call on their life and His empowerment to complete the task, they were sure to fail miserably and cause more damage than good.

Part of our role should be to affirm God's call on the lives of our companions and to do everything we can to ensure their success and obedience to God's assignments. We are not to stand in their way or in any way cancel their God-given vision or tasks. There have been many companion teams that God has used mightily over the years. D. L. Moody (1837–1899) and Ira David Sankey (1840–1908) began their working relationship around 1870, and it lasted nearly thirty years. Moody was the preacher, and Sankey was his musician and songwriter. Moody had tremendous influence during his life, and many books of his sermons are available. And we still sing Sankey's songs to this day.

Paul and Timothy were also a team. Paul reminded Timothy of the gift that was given him and encouraged him to "fan it into flame": "Therefore I remind you to inflame anew the gift of God, which is in you by the putting on of my hands. For God has not given us the spirit of fear, but of power and of love and of a sound mind. Therefore you should not be ashamed of the testimony of our Lord, nor of me His prisoner. But be partaker of the afflictions of the gospel according to the power of God" (2 Tim. 1:6–8 MKJV). We are in the perfect position to encourage our companions to pursue God's agenda for their lives and to use their God-given

> **Part of our role should be to affirm God's call on the lives of our companions and to do everything we can to ensure their success and obedience to God's assignments.**

gifts for His service. They may lack self-confidence and need our prompting and pushing to venture out into ministry. But like Paul, we can identify the potential in others and help them on their way to achieving God's best for their lives.

We should remember, too, that we are also servants of the Master, and it is the Master who directs His servants. We have to assume that Christ will help us see what it is He wants to do in and through the lives of our companions, even if it means taking them from us for His purposes. Paul always wanted his companions to have great success in ministry, because it meant the kingdom was being advanced and the light was dispelling the darkness. It was not *his* kingdom they were building, but Christ's.

Look at some of the ways Paul addressed and encouraged his companions:

- "To Titus, a true son in our common faith" (Titus 1:4).

- "To Philemon our dear friend and fellow worker . . . I always thank my God as I remember you in my prayers, because I hear about your faith in the Lord Jesus and your love for all the saints . . . your love has given me great joy and encouragement" (Philem. 1:1, 4–7).

- "Don't let anyone look down on you because you are young, but set an example for the believers in speech, in life, in love, in faith and in purity . . . do not neglect your gift, which was given you through a prophetic message when the body of elders laid their hands on you" (1 Tim. 4:12,14 NIV).

To the whole church in Thessalonica, Paul said, "We continually remember before our God and Father your work produced by faith, your labor prompted by love, and your endurance inspired by hope in our Lord

Jesus Christ" (1 Thess. 1:3 NIV). How I pray that our companions would say the best times in their ministry were when they walked with us!

COMPANIONS HAVE NOT BEEN CALLED TO MAKE LEADERS SUCCESSFUL, BUT TO MAKE CHRIST KNOWN!

God's call and His plans for your companions may not always be the same as your plans for them. It is so important to seek God's will *together* rather than dictating to companions what *your* will is for their lives. Paul wanted Apollos to go to Corinth, but Apollos decided it was not yet time. Perhaps Apollos felt that the division in the church had not yet settled such that they would listen to him. We don't know. But Apollos's first loyalty was to Christ and to the guidance of the Spirit, not to Paul. When companions seek God together, there will be no disputes over the direction to go. Christ will give them one heart and one mind to follow Him together.

Luke did not always travel with Paul. He stayed in Philippi for seven years in between Paul's missionary journeys and later joined him on the last adventure. In fact, no companion was with Paul *all* of the time. They came and went, some staying much longer than others, and some only intersecting Paul's life for a short time. God does not send companions for your own personal benefit; He sends them because He has something for them to do and to become with you. Do not become possessive of your companions or demand that their first loyalty be to you above all else. That is blasphemy. They are first and foremost servants of God, who has the right to do anything He chooses with them at any time, period!

> **Do not become possessive of your companions or demand that their first loyalty be to you above all else. That is blasphemy.**

Second, they have a loyalty to their spouses and families. The leader may, in fact, be quite far down the list, depending on the companions' core values (God, family, church, ministry, work, etc.). There may even be a time when companions must choose between loyalty to a pastor and devotion to the church body if they feel there is a conflict and the welfare of the body is at stake. But this should never happen if the pastor, his staff, and the congregation are all seeking the mind of Christ together. Unfortunately, this is not always the case.

It may be that your companions are called to more prominent ministries and tasks than you are called to. It would be wise for you to encourage, bless, and support them. Jealousy and pride can ruin great friendships. There is no indication that Barnabas ever felt slighted or overlooked because of Paul's prominence (after all, it was Paul who was stoned in Lystra, not Barnabas!). When pride and jealousy rear their ugly heads, our usefulness in ministry begins to diminish. Like John the Baptist, if God calls our companions to places of prominence, we can say with true love and respect, "He must increase, but I must decrease" (John 3:30). The key is to remember that the greater the demands God places on His servants in ministry, the more important companions are going to be.

Though we cannot draw this next point from Paul's life, it is important to see our spouses and possibly even our children among our primary companions as they begin to respond to God. It is crucial for a husband and wife to share the visions and dreams God has given them so that they can help each other achieve those dreams together. The husband does not have the right to cancel the lifelong dreams and ministry visions of the wife simply because he wants her unqualified support for his own ambitions. Peter reminds us (1 Peter 3:7) that a husband's treatment of his wife could have a direct impact on whether or not God will even hear his prayers. This is extremely important in ministry. For God to not hear our prayers because of how we have treated one whom He has sent is a very serious matter. Remember Christ's words: "He who receives whomever I send receives Me. And he who receives Me receives Him who sent Me" (John 13:20 MKJV).

Paul never used people for his own purposes or to accomplish his own goals. He always saw each person as the incarnation of Christ, called of God. It was his goal to help them experience the fullness of Christ in their lives and to live worthy of the calling as Christians. This is the attitude of a true servant of God.

COMPANIONS SHOULD NOT SEE YOU AS A HERO OR SOLE SOURCE OF SPIRITUAL GROWTH

No one person can be everything you need. No single person has all the abilities and character traits that will complement your ministry. Christ is the only hero we need as Christians, and He is enough. We are His servants, not the masters of others. Paul said, "Follow my example, as I follow the example of Christ" (1 Cor. 11:1 NIV). This shows that he, too, was a servant of the Lord and was always under the direction and guidance of Jesus, his Master. Paul was content to be a "father in the faith" to new converts and young companions, but he never presented himself other than what he was, though he certainly had the opportunity to do so more than once.

When the crowds in Lystra wanted to worship Barnabas and Paul as Zeus and Hermes (Acts 14:11–13), Paul and Barnabas were horrified and tore their clothes in anguish. I fear there are pastors and ministry leaders who would just as soon have the priests offer the sacrifices to them and be worshiped by those serving under them. The fact is, we should be greatly humbled when God determines we can be entrusted with companions. We should stand before Him and ask what He wants to teach them through our relationship with them, for we will be held accountable by their Master for our stewardship of their lives while in our care.

When Marilynn and I were engaged, I clearly recognized that God was granting me a lifelong companion. So I asked her to tell me all the vows she had ever made to God before we met. God takes very seriously every vow and commitment we make to Him (Eccl. 5:4–5; Isa. 19:21). God's blessing of our marriage and our ministry together would depend upon whether or not we fulfilled those commitments we had made to God. We would help each other faithfully fulfill each one. We have done this for each other, and God has blessed our home.

It is always flattering for people to look up to us as role models, but you and I know we are only human and come complete with character flaws, bad habits, and weaknesses no one would want to copy. When companions work together as a team, neither one needs to be in a subservient role, because the results are due to both working equally together under the leadership of God and in the power of the Holy Spirit.

WHEN A COMPANION DISAPPOINTS

There have been times when those who called themselves my friends and sought to be my companions have disappointed me. A friend who is a companion greatly helps the leader by what he does, not merely by what he says (John 15:14). Demas and Alexander would not have been able to hurt Paul so much (2 Tim. 4:10, 14) unless they had first been friends. Paul expressed his deep grief over the loss of these relationships. In the same passage he spoke of his friends deserting him in his first defense (2 Tim. 4:16).

People, even close friends, can change. Their hearts can be drawn away to many things that compete for their affections and lead them down a path that is destructive. God knows full well that disloyalty always begins in the heart: "If your heart turns away . . . and if you are drawn away . . . you will certainly be destroyed" (Deut. 30:17–18 NIV).

In an interesting set of verses from Psalm 55, David lamented not only the loss of a friendship, but the treason of Ahithophel, a trusted advisor, as he plotted David's downfall with Absalom:

Wickedness is in the midst thereof: deceit and guile depart not from her streets. For it was not an enemy that reproached me; then I could have borne it: neither was it he that hated me that did magnify himself against me; then I would have hid myself from him: But it was thou, a man mine equal, my guide, and mine [friend]. We took sweet counsel together, and walked unto the house of God in company. Let death [come suddenly to] them, and let them go down quick into hell; for wickedness is in their dwelling, and among them. As for me, I will call upon God; and the LORD shall save me. (Ps. 55:11–16 KJV)

David provided good advice. Go to God. God is the One who vindicates. He will uphold your integrity if and when the accusations come.

Praying for the restoration of the relationship and the reconciliation between friends should be a priority in your life as it was in the life of Paul: "All this is from God, who reconciled us to himself through Christ and gave us the ministry of reconciliation" (2 Cor. 5:18 NIV). The law of reciprocity says that we can affect how God treats us by how we treat others. The reverse is also true: how God treats us, we ought to treat others. As we have been forgiven, so we should forgive. As Christ intercedes on our behalf, so should we, too, intercede on behalf of our brother or sister in Christ. Few things will cause your heart more pain than to see a friend, companion, or coworker begin to face the consequences of his or her sin.

On several occasions I have been asked to give a reference for those who had previously slandered my reputation and publicly questioned my integrity. Their actions hurt me because we had worked together and had seen God bless in so many ways. But for whatever reason, their hearts toward me changed and they became critical of me and opposed to anything I was a part of. So when the requests for references came, I had a decision to make. Would I get even with them? Would I cause them as much grief as they caused me? Certainly I could malign their characters or reputations if I chose to. But I had to ask myself, what would Jesus do if He had to respond to the request?

I believe I have an obligation to those requesting my reference to be honest and forthright, yet I do not have the right to slander another person's character. Should I blithely send off the reference with vagaries and generalities, I would do the church or ministry a grave injustice, and my integrity could fairly be questioned. At the same time, a person's actions reveal what is in his or her heart, and I knew I could not in good conscience endorse someone whose heart does not exhibit Christlikeness, grace, and compassion toward others. That being said, there have been occasions when I have given a positive reference for people who have harmed me in the past and have even mentioned God's strengths in their lives. I came to the realization that Christ's model prayer in Matthew 6:12 (ISV) and His announcement recorded in Mark 11:25–26 (CEV), listed respectively, made more sense than did vengeance:

. . . and forgive us our sins, as we have forgiven those who have sinned against us.

Whenever you stand up to pray, you must forgive what others have done to you. Then your Father in heaven will forgive your sins.

However, there are times when one is obligated to warn others of one whose characters or credentials are flawed. The Scripture testifies that Paul did not hesitate to warn churches against those who had destructive intentions when their unity or safety was an issue: "Demas loves the things of this world so much that he left me . . . Alexander, the metal-worker, has hurt me in many ways . . . Alexander opposes what we preach. You had better watch out for him" (2 Tim. 4:10, 14–15 CEV).

COMPANIONS THAT REFRESH

We don't know Paul's exact age, but if he was older and seasoned, it would be interesting to see the impact of Timothy or John Mark on his life. A young, excited, idealistic youth can bring new life and hope to the older, seasoned, and often weary servants of God. The friendship between them developed to the point where Paul received pure joy when he heard of their successes and the work God was doing through them. My son Tom and I have had several companions over the years that were truly refreshing to be around. Their positive spirits and genuine faith in God brought hope and joy when we could have been cynical. It was easy for us to see these persons as true gifts from God who refreshed our hearts and emboldened our spirits. From the life of Paul, it is fair to look to those whom we lead to Christ as potential companions. Our responsibility to disciple, train, equip, and model for our new converts is enormous, yet what we receive in return can be incalculable.

I have already mentioned our formation of a training school for young pastors-to-be. Nothing will keep a veteran minister sharper than teaching theology to young men and women. They have incredible questions and insights that often surprise and delight the teacher. What an encourage-ment it is to watch young people get excited about God and His activity in their lives. Teaching and training God's people have always been a joy to me, and though it has often been demanding, it has been even more rewarding to see my students apply the truths in their own ministries.

Tom spent fifteen years as a youth minister and had the opportunity to disciple and encourage hundreds of teenagers. Few things bring more delight to him than receiving a phone call or letter from one of his former teenagers years later telling him he or she is now in ministry and thanking him for the influence he had been on that youth's life.

WHO CHOOSES WHOM?

Some companions are directed by God to walk with leaders in ministry. Some leaders are directed by God to seek out companions to complement their ministries. Other companions are natural colleagues throughout life who are in the same occupation, have been longtime friends, or may even be relatives. When my oldest son, Richard, finally graduated from seminary and went to pastor his first church, he realized that although he had many ministry strengths, there were also weak areas in which he needed help. When he looked across the field of workers for someone to serve with him, one who had the skills and background the church required, he led the church to call his brother Tom as his associate pastor.

Tom says his job was to be "Associate Pastor of Everything" because there was so much to do. But Richard never had a more loyal companion than his brother. They have both since moved from that church in Winnipeg to other ministries, but some members there still remember their time together as the "Camelot years," when God was at work and the members enjoyed sweet fellowship together.

It is not as important *where* companions come from as it is to recognize that they all are sent to you by God. Identifying when God is sending you a companion will be the key to a long and fruitful ministry. It is also important to remember that a companion may not be for life but only to help you through a particular time or situation in your life. I am at a loss to find anyone who was with Paul for his entire ministry. Companions came for a season and left, or remained in certain locations for a period of time before rejoining him.

Companions may or may not be physically with you to have a great impact on your life and ministry. The work that Paul's companions did to continue the ministries he began is a testimony to their heart and conviction for God's churches. Barnabas brought Paul into ministry, then moved on to work with others. Aquila and Priscilla helped Paul begin a church in Ephesus but did not travel with him to the many other churches. Epaphroditus joined Paul in his Roman imprisonment but was not sent as a messenger to the churches as Tychicus, Silas, or Timothy were. Companions may be brought for very specific situations to offer wisdom and godly counsel or to encourage or exhort.

> **Companions may or may not be physically with you to have a great impact on your life and ministry.**

SOME CHARACTERISTICS TO LOOK FOR IN A COMPANION

It is crucial to remember that companions bring far more to a relationship than simply ministry skills. You are not just hiring a good musician, song leader, children's worker, or administrator; you are calling a person with character, integrity, and personality who can add an incredible amount to your life, not just your ministry.

1. God-sent companions will have God-centered lives. This was true of all of Paul's companions. There were none who traveled with Paul who were not completely cognizant of God's presence and hand upon their lives. They knew and recognized God's activity in and around their lives. A godly companion will clearly see God's hand at work and affirm His action in your life. They are also able to recognize when what you think

you have heard from the Lord is clearly from God. They need the assurance of God's hand on your life for them to be a faithful and supportive companion to you.

2. A companion will be certain of the lordship of Christ in your life and in his or her own life. This common commitment to Christ as Lord will give you and your companion one heart, one mind, and one soul as you walk together with your common Lord: "Now I beseech you, brethren, for the Lord Jesus Christ's sake, and for the love of the Spirit, that ye strive together with me in your prayers to God for me" (Rom. 15:30 KJV). "Therefore, brethren, we were comforted over you in all our affliction and distress by your faith: for now we live, if ye stand fast in the Lord" (1 Thess. 3:7–8 KJV).

3. Since God's goal for each believer is "predestined to be conformed to the likeness of His Son" (Rom. 8:29 NIV), you will recognize one God has sent when the likeness of Christ is obvious in his or her life. One Scripture that can help you is Philippians 2:5–8. Paul urged believers to "let this mind be in you which was also in Christ Jesus." The verse goes on to tell us exactly what we are to emulate from Christ's example:

- Christ never clung to His "rights."
- Christ took on Him the form of a bond servant.
- Christ was made in the likeness of man, that is, took on Him the form of those He came to serve and to save.
- Christ humbled Himself.
- Christ became obedient even to death.
- Christ laid down His life in love, even to taking up His cross.

4. A companion must be one who believes God at all times and has walked faithfully with Him. When facing circumstances that call for great faith, such companions are indispensable. Paul often spoke of the faith in his companions as being a great strength and encouragement to him and the work of God's kingdom. When a person has these servant qualities, you will know God has sent that one to you.

5. Practically, note how faithful they have been in other assignments. If a person has only stayed one to one and a half years in five or six of his last places of service, avoid him. He is too unstable in doing the will of God regardless of his "explanations." A long obedience in the same direction is a desirable characteristic of a companion. Faithfulness to the task regardless of the circumstances denotes strong character and a stable attitude toward ministry.

6. Look for a companion to be teachable. Some may come with all the answers to everything and feel God wants them to be with you. Avoid a person who is obviously not teachable. He or she will always be talking and never listening. Such a person will never be able to learn from his or her mistakes and the mistakes of others. A companion who listens, who asks many questions in order to learn, and who is willing to adjust to circumstances will be a great asset in ministry.

7. Another characteristic of a strong companion is flexibility. One who is living in his *comfort zone* could never have been Paul's companion. This flexibility should also include "taking up his cross daily"—the willingness to stay faithful when criticized and suffering. Paul desired to know, by experience, the "fellowship of Christ's suffering," especially in helping the churches (Col. 1:24–25; Phil. 3:10). A person who continually complains when ministry is difficult or it costs something is not ready

to be a companion to God's servants. Paul's life was not orderly and planned. It often required spontaneous action and a change of plans according to the leadership of the Spirit, or the circumstances that he faced. Flexibility requires a high degree of trust in God and the belief that He is in control regardless of any situation a person faces.

GOD'S AGENDA THROUGH COMPANIONS

When you realize that God does nothing by accident and that He has a very clear purpose in mind when He provides companions to you, you need to ask:

- What is it that God wants to do in my life through my companion?
- Is there some refining that needs to take place in my life?
- Are there some truths my companion has learned that I need to learn?
- Is there a situation coming in the next year that will require the help of my companion?
- How can I treat my companion as though he were Christ, sent by God, to me?
- Are there Scriptures I need to be praying into my companion's life to prepare him [or her] for present and future ministries?

I recommend spending much time in prayer over your companions and not taking them for granted. If God has sent companions to you, it would be wise to ask Him what He has in mind. Certainly He means to help you in *your* work, but also, you are to help them in *their* work.

The Old Testament reminds us, "Two are better than one, because they have a good reward for their labor. For if they fall, one will lift up his companion. But woe to him who is alone when he falls, for he has no one to help him up" (Eccl. 4:9–10). With so many pastors and leaders falling into sin and losing their ministries (no one to lift them up), it is vital for every leader to receive carefully and prayerfully any godly companion God may give him or her. Most that I know about who have fallen had no close companions to walk with them.

God also reminds us that we need companions to keep us alert and growing and good stewards of His great salvation: "As iron sharpens iron, so a man sharpens the countenance of his friend" (Prov. 27:17). The presence of a God-given companion is a great stimulus to grow in our relationship with God and to have a fruitful ministry. Paul affirmed this in his relationship with Apollos:

Who then is Paul, and who is Apollos, but ministers through whom you believed, as the Lord gave to each one? I planted, Apollos watered, but God gave the increase . . . Now he who plants and he who waters are one, and each one will receive his own reward according to his own labor. For we are God's fellow workers. (1 Cor. 3:5–6, 8–9).

Paul knew that he was not a "one-man show" and that God had called others to play a significant role in helping to plant, water, and grow churches. There have been many times when I have sought out the advice of others, or asked companions of mine to pray with me over various situations or decisions I have had to make. Seeking out others in times of need or decision-making is one way to use the resources God has placed around you. In this way, each person benefits from the strengths and insights of one another, and everyone can rejoice together in the fruit of your labor.

STUDY QUESTIONS

1. There is a loyalty and a deep bonding between a new convert and the one who leads him or her to the Lord. If you are not leading others to Christ, are you denying yourself access to potential companions in your later years?

2. Paul had to wait months to receive any word from close friends and coworkers to see if they were alive or to find out how God was using them. Today there is an unprecedented ability to communicate over vast distances and to stay in constant contact with one another. The quick and easy modes of transportation and communication mean that it is possible to play a very important role in the lives of people without being physically present. Paul's deep love for others combined with the long distances between them resulted in fervent prayer in tears for his companions and for the fledgling churches. In return, he often requested their prayers on his behalf. Do you demonstrate your love for the ones God has sent you by interceding on their behalf and by requesting their prayers for you?

3. The Holy Spirit still remains the major factor in companionship, in choosing and directing and bringing them together. Is it possible that you are grieving the Holy Spirit by not accepting those He is sending to you in ministry?

4. What happens when you differ with your companions? God calls us to be reconcilers. Those who try to use Paul's treatment of Mark as an excuse for breaking fellowship and leaving people behind in ministry have never read the rest of the story. They fail to realize that Paul's relationship extended past the initial disappointment and rejection of John Mark, and on to a very close, brotherly love between the two. In 2 Timothy 4:11, Paul says, "Get Mark and bring him with you, for he is useful to me for ministry." Are there relationships that need mending and reconciliation in your past or current ministries? Can you see that how you have treated your past companions and colleagues is also how you have treated Christ?

5. List the companions God has given to you, at very particular times in your life, who brought the skill or character traits you needed.

SEVEN

BEING A COMPANION TO GOD'S SERVANTS

BEING THE ONE GOD sends is not always an easy role to have, but it is almost always extremely rewarding. I have often wondered what it would have been like to be a companion to Christ during the three years of His earthly ministry. To sit at His feet, watch the incredible power of God flowing through Him, and have my mind stretched to overflowing with the truths He spoke would be a dream come true. Or to walk with Paul along the dusty roads of Asia Minor, discussing theology, church growth, and the incredible grace of God, would have been a life-transforming experience for anyone. But not every position as a companion is so rewarding.

There may be times when being a companion will bring difficult challenges that force a deeper dependence on God. A companion may question his call to ministry and whether he should ever have answered the call in the first place. My son Tom once told me that, twice in his life, people he worked with had informed him that he had no future in ministry and that he should pursue a secular line of work. But the past twenty years of successful ministry he now has under his belt would seem to prove his critics wrong. Because Tom chose to believe God's call rather than listen to a few critical people, thousands of lives have been impacted as God continues to work through his life and his writing.

Not many of us would want to be Elisha as he tried to work with the reclusive Elijah (1 Kings 19:16–21). Elijah had lost heart for the work of God, and his time was coming to an end. Just keeping up with Elijah seemed to be quite the challenge at the very end. Elijah rebuffed him and discouraged him from following him, but Elisha accepted the challenge, persevered, and earned the right to be Elijah's successor (2 Kings 2:1–15). Though it was apparent that Elijah wanted no companions, it was God's call on Elisha that mattered.

It is right to admire Paul for his faithfulness and to want to be like him in ministry. However, God chose Paul for a very special task, and our roles in God's kingdom are going to be different. Many of us will be given the assignment to be a companion to others in ministry. What that looks like depends on your calling, experience, and obedience to God's call on your life.

When we look at Paul's life, we see a variety of ways people related to him as his companions and just as many ways Paul related to them as their companion. Knowing it is Christ you are serving is the key to being a companion to one of God's servants. Service to others is one of the great ambitions in Christ's kingdom (Matt. 20:20–28; 23:11–12). In fact, the better you are as a servant, the more influence your life will have. I believe that was the key to Paul's success: the ability to be a servant to those he was leading. *Greatness in serving* should be the motto of every companion, because it keeps the focus on Christ and off of self.

HAVING THE RIGHT ATTITUDE

One of the requirements Christ had for His followers is found in Matthew 16:24: "If anyone desires to come after Me, let him deny himself, and take up his cross, and follow Me." Here we see three actions:

1. Denying self

2. Taking up one's cross

3. Following [Him]

None of us naturally desires to do this; it is the work of the Holy Spirit in our hearts that enables us to put others first, to accept whatever God brings to us, and to obey whatever commands or assignments He gives to us. When applying this verse to companionship, we can discern several principles. In *denying self* we put others first. The one to whom we have become a companion becomes the focus of our prayers, our good intentions, our blessings, and our energetic support. These things are sometimes not deserved; neither may the one we are called to serve even appreciate them, but they are required for you to be a good companion.

David was brought into the service of a paranoid, psychotic king who regularly tried to take his life. Try functioning in that setting!

David was brought into the service (1 Sam. 18:2) of a paranoid, psychotic king who regularly tried to take his life (1 Sam. 18:9–12). Try functioning in that setting! Yet in his heart of hearts he knew that the king had been selected by God and anointed by Samuel, and for David to wish any harm to the king would be an affront to God (1 Sam. 24:6). He worked at every assignment with all his strength and wisdom and became loved by all who knew and worked with him (1 Sam. 18:5). His loyalty to the king was noticed by everyone and affected their attitude toward the king and toward David.

Now, I know that some associate staff feel that the one they have been called to work with may have Saul-like tendencies toward them, or at least minor psychotic episodes. Even so, one's integrity before God and those watching his or her life is paramount to one's success. I can't help but think of David's encounters with Nabal and his wife, Abigail (1 Sam. 18). Nabal insulted David and his soldiers and brought upon himself a death sentence because of it. Yet despite having a foolish and worthless (1 Sam. 25:25) husband, Abigail acted wisely and saved the lives of her household. Her actions were duly noted, and she was rewarded for her sensible dealings (1 Sam. 25:33–34, 42). This Old Testament story demonstrates how a companion can bring blessing to others despite the cowardly or arrogant actions of the one to whom he or she is attached. One who denies self, takes up his cross, and follows Christ can act in ways that are pleasing to Christ and that benefit others regardless of the character of those over him in ministry.

Some problematic pastors have associates who have become the de facto pastors to the rest of the staff because of their gentle spirits and servant hearts. They bring peace to a troubled staff situation and offer wise counsel to their colleagues. The senior pastors are respected and feared, but not loved and appreciated. In such a case, the pastor has become the preacher, CEO, and chief administrator of the organization, but the associate, the companion to the pastor, has taken on the role of servant and pastor to the staff and many of the congregation. In several cases, the associate is then called to serve in senior positions in other churches because everyone notices his or her integrity, servant's heart, and hard work. David's character and reputation went far when he became king over Israel. The loyalty and respect from the people were already there because they had been watching him respond in very difficult circumstances for years.

THE COMPANIONSHIP OF PAUL

Paul demonstrated a keen understanding of what it means to be a companion. He was a great encourager of those he worked with. Look at what he said to believers in the churches in Rome and Corinth:

- "I myself am convinced, my brothers, that you yourselves are full of goodness, complete in knowledge and competent to instruct one another. I have written you quite boldly on some points, as if to remind you of them again, because of the grace God gave me" (Rom. 15:14).

- "I will very gladly spend and be spent for your souls; though the more abundantly I love you, the less I am loved" (2 Cor. 12:15). (Paul did not wait for others to love him or respect and honor him before he gave his love to them.)

- "We are glad whenever we are weak but you are strong; and our prayer is for your perfection . . . aim for perfection, listen to my appeal, be of one mind, live in peace. And the God of love and peace will be with you" (2 Cor. 13:9–11 NIV).

- Regarding Titus, Paul said, "I begged Titus and sent with him the brother. Did Titus overreach you? Did we not walk in the same spirit? Did we not walk in the same steps?" (2 Cor. 12:18 MKJV).

I think too often companions to leaders forget that they, too, are leading others. Whether it is your own family or an entire wing of an organization, companions to others are also leaders in their own right. Paul was keenly aware of this and lived his life so that if anyone followed him, there would be nothing in his life that would cause him or her to stumble or fall. With all honesty Paul could say, "Whatever you have learned or received or heard from me, or seen in me—put it into practice" (Phil. 4:9 NIV). Further, Paul was convinced that because Christ could consider him worth saving, anyone could be saved. He would not treat anyone with any less regard than Christ would: "Accept one another then, just as Christ accepted you, in order to bring praise to God" (Rom. 15:7 NIV).

There are two great things for which you as a companion should pray when God brings you together with a leader. First, ask God to help you discern what He has put in your life that can be used to encourage the other person. And second, ask the Holy Spirit to create a sensitive heart to listen for how He wants to use your life to impact the leader with whom you are colaboring.

WORKING WITH DIFFICULT LEADERS

Though being a companion of Paul would have been very demanding, I do not see Paul as a difficult person to walk with. His heart of compassion and grace shines too brightly through his letters for us to imagine him as harsh, critical, or demanding. But we have mentioned a few examples of difficult leaders in the Old Testament. The tragic relationship between David and King Saul provides us with some principles worth exploring.

Should you . . . work with a difficult leader, seek to learn all you can about yourself and about God; there may be some very important lessons God needs to teach you.

Should you find yourself in the position of having to work with a difficult leader, seek to learn all you can about yourself and about God; there may be some very important lessons God needs to teach you. A seminary president once confided in me that he had a very large amount of money to raise in only a few months' time to meet his budget. Then he recounted to me the last prayer time he had with his staff, when he was greatly encouraged by the prayer of one of his professors. Instead of asking God for money, donations, or support, the man prayed *thanking* God that He had allowed them to get into the place where they were now totally dependent upon Him. What an incredible insight; what remarkable faith!

When God places one of His people at the side of a difficult leader, it is important that he or she has security in his or her own calling. This enables that companion to walk alongside such a demanding leader with patience and integrity. If this is you, then knowing that it is God you are serving can help soften the frustration you may face. Have faith that God may have elected to use you to impact the leader's life. Are you ready to act as Abigail did and show the contrast between godly integrity and self-ish ambition? Do you have the wherewithal to wait patiently, as David did, for God to bring a blessing to your life and resist the temptation to take matters into your own hands?

I heard about a woman who had previously been in a difficult work situation and had sent out a stack of résumés to get free from it. There was no prayer involved in her decision to pursue a career in another city. She never looked back when she left her job, because she felt free from the trouble. But as soon as she arrived in her new location, she knew it was a huge mistake. The next few years of her life were the most miserable of all her career. She knew clearly that she was outside God's will for her life. Now she wondered what it was that God had wanted her to learn in the troubled company where she'd been and what truths about God she had missed by running from God's will.

Difficult circumstances refine our characters and reveal what is in our hearts. Troubling times are growing times:

> We were under great pressure, far beyond our ability to endure, so that we despaired even of life. Indeed, in our hearts we felt the sentence of death. But this happened that we might not rely on ourselves but on God, who raises the dead. He has delivered us from such a deadly peril, and he will deliver us. On him we have set our hope that he will continue to deliver us, as you help us by your prayers. (2 Cor. 1:8–11 NIV)

No one can look at the life of Joseph or Daniel without realizing the incredible rewards one receives when he or she remains faithful in difficult times.

Difficulties or weaknesses in others are not to be used for criticism, but for intercession. This is especially true for a companion. God may have called you as an intercessor on behalf of the one you are working with.

Here is a good verse to consider when praying for your leader: "Jerusalem, on your walls I have stationed guards, whose duty it is to speak out day and night, without resting. They must remind the LORD and not let him rest till he makes Jerusalem strong and famous everywhere" (Isa. 62:6–7 CEV). Can you commit to *not resting* until God makes your leader strong and famous everywhere? (Here, we mean strong in the Lord, rather than in man's strength.) When the Lord makes a man *strong and famous*, it is because he has been obedient to Him, not because he is a talented speaker or gifted musician.

Will you commit to praying as Paul did, for your leader? "Night and day we pray most earnestly that we may see you again and supply what is lacking in your faith" (1 Thess. 3:10 NIV). Sometimes we give up on people because we do not want to take the time to invest in helping them become what God needs them to be. We expect perfection from them, but God brought us alongside *raw material* that needs His shaping and refining.

You say, "That's not my job! I'm the assistant [or associate]." Your job is whatever God tells you it is. You are the servant of God Almighty, who has selected you to be the iron that sharpens iron, the friend who sticks closer than a brother, the fellow prisoner and yokefellow in Christ. Paul did not give up on John Mark because of his initial failures. He came to Mark's side as an encourager and supporter.

Another reason God may have brought you alongside a difficult leader may be that there is a message He wants you to share with that leader. If God asks you to be a Nathan, do not be afraid (2 Sam. 12:1–14).

You may save a man's career, a ministry, a family, and a marriage by speaking truth in love at the right time. "But [you], speaking the truth in love, may grow up in all things into Him who is the head—Christ—from whom the whole body, joined and knit together by what every joint supplies, according to the effective working by which every part does its share, causes growth of the body for the edifying of itself in love" (Eph. 4:15–16).

God may have given you spiritual insights that must be shared with your leader. It is your obligation as a servant of God's to share the truths God gives you. Had Nathan not spoken to King David and caused him to face his sin, a kingdom would have been lost. The temple would not have been built. The fate of the coming Messiah would have been jeopardized. You can speak truth to a leader when you have a clear understanding that it is God whom you serve.

If you have let your pastor, executive, team leader, or organizational founder become god to you, you will have difficulty with this task. Taking a moral or ethical stand is never an easy thing to do, but to not take a stand will have far more devastating consequences in the long run. One note of caution though: do not try to *play God* in another person's life by doing what only God has the right or the ability to do. You are the messenger, not the Holy Spirit. Wagging judgmental fingers never seems to have quite the same lasting impact as weeping together over a person's sin. You will have to trust God to work for His purposes in the leader's life through you, for God's Spirit is always at work in the lives of His people.

One messenger paid the ultimate price for telling the truth. John the Baptist was imprisoned and killed for exposing corruption and sin at the top of society. Realize that you may become the object of attack out of jealousy or because your life may cause great feelings of guilt or inadequacy in your leader. Some leaders have significant insecurities that lead them to ungodly and, at times, irrational behavior. King Saul is at the top of the list! He drove away all of his God-given companions, and he died

Realize that you may become the object of attack out of jealousy or because your life may cause great feelings of guilt or inadequacy in your leader.

alone, far away from what God had intended for his life. So disastrous was his fall that it took the life of his own son, David's trusted friend and companion, Prince Jonathan.

Your leader may try to slander your character, openly criticize you, give you ultimatums, or outright fire you. But your good character and your integrity, as well as your faithful trust in God, will see you through. Persecution of God's people is not always carried out by lost people. Sometimes carnal Christians can be just as ruthless against their brothers and sisters in Christ as non-Christians can be. The apostle Paul endured slander, criticism, and ridicule by immature, self-serving, and arrogant people in Corinth (1 Cor. 3:1; 4:18). When Paul said, "When we are cursed, we bless; when we are persecuted, we endure it; when we are slandered, we answer kindly" (1 Cor. 4:12–13 NIV), I am not sure whether he referred to worldly opposition or attacks from believers. But regardless of the source, his response would have been the same.

CALLED TO A RELATIONSHIP—NOT A JOB

I therefore, the prisoner of the Lord, beseech you to walk worthy of the calling with which you were called, with all lowliness and gentleness, with long-suffering, bearing with one another in love, endeavoring to keep the unity of the Spirit in the bond of peace. (Eph. 4:1–3)

My son Tom was shocked to hear a conference speaker once say, "Staff are called to a *pastor*, not to a *church*." This went against everything he had learned about his relationship with God. Tom could not understand how staff could be *called to a pastor*. Does this mean when the pastor leaves, you are obligated to go with him wherever he goes? If the pastor tries to lead you to do what you sense is against God's will, do you blindly obey? What happens to your call if the pastor fires you? Can he cancel God's call on your life? This type of thinking has created all sorts of problems in ministry organizations today.

You see, God does not call you to a position or a job. He calls you into a relationship with Himself. The call is to servanthood, with God as our Master. God assigns us to various tasks, ministries, and positions of service, but the call is continuous and irrevocable. Your call to a relationship with God will be the one constant in a life of service.

I began ministry as a part-time education/music minister while in seminary in California. From there I served as a pastor, Bible school president, director of missions, denominational worker, and now ministry leader. Which one of those was I "called" to? None. I was called to a relationship with a living Lord, who assigned places of ministry to which I was to be faithful. In each place of service, God taught me, molded me and grew me in my understanding of Him. He is the Master; I am the servant. If you can understand that your call is to know God and be obedient to whatever task or ministry He assigns you, you will have a heart to know Him and to serve Him regardless of your situation.

It has always been curious to me when people come to me and ask me to "put in a good word" for them to their bosses or superiors, as though what I say would make life easier for them somehow. The request tells me more about the person asking it than it does about their boss. I feel sad that such people have not learned to trust in God and instead look to others to intervene on their behalf. I am sure there are plenty of people who are frustrated with their leaders, but the moment you take your eyes off of God and His plan and call for your life, you are taking matters into your own hands. Politicking, maneuvering, and scheming among God's people has no place in the kingdom of God and can quickly remove God's blessing.

> **Politicking, maneuvering, and scheming among God's people has no place in the kingdom of God and can quickly remove God's blessing.**

We see in David's life a man who would not sacrifice his own integrity despite the despicable behavior of King Saul. David's integrity was not for sale or for compromise. When Paul wrote 1 Corinthians 13 (often called "the love chapter"), he wanted to describe both what God is like and what His people should look like. When he wrote about the fruit of the Spirit in Galatians 5:22–23, he had in mind how love would work itself out in our lives. It is easy to demonstrate these characteristics in times of peace and quiet, but the real measure is how we do in the midst of conflict and stress. Watch God develop your character through the difficult circumstances.

One of the most difficult things to do when facing a difficult leader is to love him. But isn't that what we are to do as servants of Christ's? Read the following verses from John's letter (NIV):

- "God is love. Whoever lives in love lives in God, and God in him . . . Love is made complete among us so that we will have confidence on the day of judgment, because in this world we are like him. There is no fear in love. But perfect love drives out fear" (1 John 4:16–18).

- "Anyone who does not love his brother, whom he has seen, cannot love God, whom he has not seen" (1 John 4:20b).

- "Anyone who does not do what is right is not a child of God; nor is anyone who does not love his brother" (1 John 3:10b).

Be certain that you do not lose Christ's love for the leader. Love him as Christ loves him, and let Christ continue to love him *through you*. Love does not mean that you necessarily *like* the person or his behavior. In fact, you may have no respect for him whatsoever. But it *does* mean that you wish God's very best for him and that you will do what you can to bring it about in his life, regardless of how he responds to you.

QUALITIES OF A GODLY COMPANION

If we walk in the light as He is in the light, we have fellowship with one another. (1 John 1:7)

The only way we are going to have fellowship with our companions in ministry is if we walk in the light of God's Word and His presence and function in the light of the Spirit's power. Because God has initiated our ministry, it is essential that we maintain our relationship with God so that our relationship with others will be kept in proper perspective. When we encourage, admonish, or seek to inspire our companions, it is important that what we say is derived from our time with God. These are all the results of God's Word at work in our own lives (2 Tim. 3:16–17). It is fascinating to realize that many of Paul's exhortations to his companions and other believers became Scriptures to be used for the same purposes with our own companions.

We should not be given to jealousy or envy but should rejoice with our companions in their successes and weep with them in times of distress. "Let nothing be done through selfish ambition or conceit, but in lowliness of mind let each esteem others better than himself. Let each of you look out not only for his own interests, but also for the interest of others" (Phil. 2:3).

Associates who undermine the pastor in order to replace him do not follow this Scripture. Unfortunately, there are those who cannot wait for

God to give them places of ministry with more recognition, so they seek them out for themselves. Paul called this selfish ambition, and it is one of the most dangerous character flaws a companion can possess. Paul was well aware of those who sought their own advancement over others: "I know that after I leave, savage wolves will come in among you and will not spare the flock. Even from your own number men will arise and distort the truth in order to draw away disciples after them" (Acts 20:29–30 NIV).

We are to have genuine love for God and for our companions: "This is how we know what love is: Jesus Christ laid down his life for us. And we ought to lay down our lives for our brothers" (1 John 3:16 NIV). A person cannot read through the letters of Paul without seeing how deeply he loved those to whom he wrote. Companions serve out of love, not obligation, duty, or loyalty. "Love will cover a multitude of sins" (1 Peter 4:8). God says, "Whoever loves [Me] must also love his brother" (1 John 4:21 NIV). It takes some time to develop the kind of relationship Paul had with his companions. But the strain and stress they faced together deepened their bonds of love for one another and for the churches they strove to encourage, so much so that Paul could write, "I have said before that you have such a place in our hearts that we would live or die with you" (2 Cor. 7:3 NIV).

> Unfortunately, there are those who cannot wait for God to give them places of ministry with more recognition, so they seek them out for themselves.

Every companion, every Christian, should have the personal goal of exhibiting the fruit of the Spirit in his or her life (Gal. 5:22–23). Love, joy, peace, long-suffering (patience), kindness, goodness, faithfulness, gentleness, and self-control are qualities that are indispensable when working with others. Knowing that you are to be *Christ* to others, and knowing that you are to treat those with whom you work as though they are *Christ*, enables you to better focus on these qualities. Can you say these qualities are dominant in your life, or do pride, jealousy, selfish ambition, anger, hatred, and desire for personal recognition rear their heads in your life? The fruit of the Spirit are all qualities the Christ demonstrated in His own life. Having these qualities is ultimately not the goal; Christlikeness is.

Sometimes companionship is costly. Are you willing to pay the price of companionship? There are many people who love to criticize those above them, and then bail out when the going gets tough. John Mark may well fit into this category. In Luke 14:28 Jesus talks about counting the cost before beginning a project. Companionship can be extremely demanding, and sacrifices are often required. Obviously one cannot predict what the costs may be at the outset of a relationship. Being a faithful companion who will not flee in the face of hardship, but will stand with firm resolve through to the other side, may not necessarily be who you are today, but it may be the person you will grow to be in the years to come.

When Paul referred to his *fellow prisoners*, he was not using this term figuratively. Silas was bound, beaten, chained, and thrown into the same rank prison cell as Paul. Epaphras and Timothy also faced the inside of the prison walls with Paul, but they stood firm and never wavered in their devotion to him. Many of Paul's companions faced beatings, shipwrecks, mob violence, and injustice, just as Paul did, with little or no fanfare or notice. It was simply a way of life for Paul and those who traveled with him. You can see why even their contemporaries held them in such high regard as heroes of the faith.

Can you describe yourself as a team player? Companions utilize synergy when they work together. That is, their work together accomplishes more than adding up their work done separately. Working together honors Christ, the Head of the church, because He has an opportunity to join you in your labor (Matt. 18:20). The team effort is not limited to just you and your companion: Christ, through His Spirit, is always present as you work together.

John Wesley was not in favor of organization. His associates did have a "United Society" who were "a company of men having the form, and seeking the power of godliness, united in order to pray together, to receive the Word of exhortation, and to watch over one another in love, that they may help each other to work out their salvation." It was because of those who followed him that "Methodism" took hold and became a powerfully influential religious organization over the years.

WHAT TO PRAY TOWARD YOUR LEADER

In his closing remarks to the Ephesian church, Paul prayed for peace, love, faith, and grace "from God the Father and the Lord Jesus Christ" (Eph. 6:23–24). To the Philippians Paul said, "And this is my prayer: that your love may abound more and more in knowledge and depth of insight, so that you may be able to discern what is best and may be pure and blameless until the day of Christ, filled with the fruit of righteousness that comes through Jesus Christ—to the glory and praise of God" (1:9–11 NIV). He reminded the Colossians:

> We have not stopped praying for you and asking God to fill you with the knowledge of his will through all spiritual wisdom and understanding. And we pray this in order that you may live a life worthy of the Lord and may please him in every way: bearing fruit in every good work, growing in the knowledge of God, being strengthened with all power according to his glorious might so that you may have great endurance and patience, and joyfully giving thanks to the Father. (1:9–12 NIV)

There are many commands Paul included throughout his writings that really should be part of a companion's repertoire of actions, many of which follow:

- "Love each other as brothers and sisters and honor others more than you do yourself" (Rom. 12:10 CEV).

- "So then let us pursue the things of peace, and the things for building up one another" (Rom. 14:19 MKJV).

- "Then we who are strong ought to bear the infirmities of the weak, and not to please ourselves. Let every one of us please his neighbor for his good, to building up. For even Christ did not please Himself; but as it is written, 'The reproaches of those who reproached You fell on Me.' For whatever things were written before were written for our learning, so that we through patience and comfort of the Scriptures might have hope. And may the God of patience and consolation grant you to be like-minded toward one another according to Christ Jesus, so that with one mind *and* one mouth you may glorify God, even the Father of our Lord Jesus Christ. Therefore receive one another as Christ also received us, to the glory of God" (Rom. 15:1–7 MKJV).

- "For I will not dare to speak of any of those things which Christ did not work out by me for the obedience of the nations in word and deed, in power of miracles and wonders, in power of the Spirit of God" (Rom. 15:18–19 MKJV).

- "Then how is it, brothers? When you come together, each one of you has a psalm, has a teaching, has a tongue, has a revelation, has an interpretation. Let all things be for building up" (1 Cor. 14:26 MKJV).

- "You know the house of Stephanas, that it is the firstfruit of Achaia, and they appointed themselves to ministry to the saints. See that you also submit to such ones" (1 Cor. 16:15–16 MKJV).

- "So then as we have time, let us work good toward all, especially toward those of the household of faith" (Gal. 6:10 MKJV).

- "And be kind to one another, tenderhearted, forgiving one another, even as God for Christ's sake has forgiven you" (Eph. 4:32 MKJV).

- "[Submit] yourselves to one another in the fear of God" (Eph. 5:21 MKJV).

- "Only let your conduct be as becomes the gospel of Christ, so that whether I come and see you, or else am absent, I may hear of your affairs, that you stand fast in one spirit, striving together with one mind for the faith of the gospel" (Phil. 1:27 MKJV).

- "I therefore, the prisoner in the Lord, beseech you that you walk worthy of the calling with which you are called, with all lowliness and meekness, with long-suffering, forbearing one another in love, endeavoring to keep the unity of the Spirit in the bond of peace" (Eph. 4:1–3 MKJV).

- "But above all these things put on love, which is the bond of perfection. And let the peace of God rule in your hearts, to which also you were called in one body; and be thankful. Let the word of Christ dwell in you richly in all wisdom, teaching and admonishing one another in psalms and hymns and spiritual songs, singing with grace in your hearts to the Lord. And whatever you do in word or deed, do all in the name of the Lord Jesus, giving thanks to God the Father through Him" (Col. 3:14–17).

- "And you became imitators of us and of the Lord, welcoming the Word in much affliction, with joy of the Holy Spirit, so that you were examples to all who believe in Macedonia and Achaia" (1 Thess. 1:6–7 MKJV).

Paul was clear in his expectations for believers both in his writings, and in person when he visited the churches. Not only did he preach them and write them down, but he lived them out just in case anyone had any doubts as to his sincerity. Paul left us his "instruction manual" for godly living, for getting along with others, and for behaving in a manner that would bring glory to God. He knew there would be great pressure to conform to the world's ways (Rom. 8:28ff) and even persecution to try and turn believers away from following Christ. Paul did everything he knew to do in order to strengthen and establish believers in their faith so that when difficult times came, they would stand firm.

STUDY QUESTIONS

1. Can you honestly say that God has called you to be a companion to one of His servants?

2. As a companion, are your motives pure and focused on what is best for your leader?

3. In what ways have you seen your character grow in the midst of working with difficult leaders? Were you impressed with your growth, or disappointed in what you discovered about yourself?

4. Make a list of the fruits of the Spirit and the acts of the flesh (Eph. 5). Place a check beside those items where God is at work building these qualities into you, as well as those things God is trying to remove from your life. Can you see "works of the flesh" that are preventing you from being the companion God wants you to be?

5. How have you honored those who look to you for guidance?

6. How successful have you been in serving Christ through your companionship to others?

7. In your role as a companion, how has God used you to impact those with whom He has placed you?

8. Can you see ways in which you may have been impatient with God and tried to take matters into your own hands as a companion to others?

9. In your own words, describe what it will mean or look like—first for yourself and then for your church—to deny self, take up your cross, and follow Christ.

10. List those to whom you have become a companion. Are these people aware of that fact?

11. What qualities has God given to you that others need for their lives?

12. List others who have become good leaders because of your friendship to them.

13. Discuss whether you feel called to a *job* or to a *relationship* with *God* as His servant.

14. Discuss what it means to "walk in the light as He is in the light" (1 John 1:7).

EIGHT

What We Can Learn from Paul and His Companions

"FOR WE ARE GOD'S WORKMANSHIP, created in Christ Jesus to do good works, which God prepared in advance for us to do" (Eph. 2:10 NIV). In this verse Paul reminds us that God created us for specific purposes and that He has planned particular involvements for each of us in His kingdom. Paul reinforced this idea to the Corinthians when, in both of his letters, he said that we are *fellow workers with God* (1 Cor. 3:9; 2 Cor. 6:1). These verses contain two different meanings. One, that we are fellow workers under God's leadership and direction, and two, that we are working together *with* God in His kingdom. In either case, we are working *together*. This is not a choice.

This is not optional or up to our discretion. This is *the* strategy in God's kingdom for accomplishing God's purposes. God's kingdom has little room for spiritual mavericks, loners, and isolationists, because every single person who names Christ as Lord is to function in community, as a part of the body of Christ.

It is so evident today that many leaders have

> **God's kingdom has little room for spiritual mavericks, loners, and isolationists.**

never known, or have simply forgotten, the corporate and interdependent nature of God's call on their lives. Each sees himself more as a "royal priest" than as a part of a "royal priesthood." Many Christians leave their churches to pursue what they believe to be God's call on their lives, forsaking God's intended interdependence for His people. If they could only see that God's eternal plan is to minister with fellow believers, their ministries would come into line with *His* purposes and *His* ways and achieve *His* results.

By the time his enemies finally silenced him, Paul had left a legacy of companions all across Asia Minor who faithfully carried on the gospel message. This was what God had intended from the beginning: "This man is my chosen instrument to carry my name before the Gentiles and their kings and before the people of Israel. I will show him how much he must suffer for me" (Acts 9:15–16 NIV). The encouraging part for Paul is that God never meant for him to do this task alone. God's plan involved surrounding him with outstanding and faithful companions to help carry the message and the load. Their undying devotion to Paul and his message continued long after Paul had gone because they had a common purpose and a common Lord.

The Scripture reveals God and His ways as He purposes to redeem a world across every generation. The book of Acts together with Paul's letters reveal not *man's* strategies, but God's. This truth must be clearly noted. Paul's ministry with God-appointed companions is God's template for ministry. This template has been developed for use in every generation to reach a world with the gospel. Yes, there are lots of ways to win people to Christ and plenty of church-planting strategies in use today. But the simple fact is, none of them, even combined, have had the worldwide impact that God had through Paul's life.

Looking back over five decades of ministry, dozens of names and faces come to mind; men and women with whom I have walked together under the lordship of Christ. I see how each of us continues to carry the message of truth to others around the world and will do so as long as we have breath. I am so grateful to God that this is also evident in the lives of my five children, who have each taken up the banner and carried it in his or her own way into their own ministries. It deeply grieves me to see the children of fellow workers and companions reject the church and God's kingdom after seeing their parents give their lives in faithful service. Sometimes children resent God and His church for taking their parents from them at crucial times in their lives. It is so important for companions to work together to encourage and support one another's families so that the legacy of ministry can continue through our children as God calls them into relationship with Him.

The Scripture says, "What will it profit a man if he gains the whole world, and loses his own soul?" (Mark 8:36). Similarly, what profit is there if a man and woman give their whole lives to ministry and lose their own family in the process? Yes, sacrifices must often be made in the name of ministry, but these hardships are meant to draw us together, not tear us apart. May God grant us the wisdom and foresight to always keep in mind those who will follow us, whether they are younger believers in the faith, or our own children.

PAUL KNEW GOD'S GRACE

Paul had a clear appreciation that everything he was and all that he had accomplished were the results of the grace of God at work in his life. He wrote to Timothy:

> I used to say terrible and insulting things about him, and I was cruel. But he had mercy on me because I didn't know what I was doing, and I had not yet put my faith in him. Christ Jesus our Lord was very kind to me. He has greatly blessed my life with faith and love just like his own. "Christ Jesus came into the world to save sinners." This saying is true, and it can

be trusted. I was the worst sinner of all! But since I was worse than anyone else, God had mercy on me and let me be an example of the endless patience of Christ Jesus. He did this so that others would put their faith in Christ and have eternal life. (1 Tim. 1:13–16 CEV)

Paul believed the very fact that he was alive was due to God's grace and that the hand of God should direct every moment of his life. "And I no longer live, but Christ lives in me. The life I live in the body, I live by faith in the Son of God, who loved me and gave himself for me" (Gal. 2:20 NIV). Because of this, Paul was not willing to set aside anything that God had done in his life that was to be used in God's service and to bring glory to Him (Gal. 2:21).

Paul had a keen awareness of the powerful activity of God's grace shaping and molding him: "But by God's grace I am what I am, and His grace toward me was not ineffective. However, I worked more than any of them, yet not I, but God's grace that was with me" (1 Cor. 15:10 HCSB). But, Paul reminds us, he had to cooperate with God's activity and not resist the work of God in his life.

Paul knew very well the price God had to pay to redeem him. His worst nightmare was for God to have wasted His efforts on him.

Paul knew very well the price God had to pay to redeem him. His worst nightmare was for God to have wasted His efforts on him. To the Corinthians Paul wrote, "Working together with Him, we also appeal to you: 'Don't receive God's grace in vain'" (2 Cor. 6:1 HCSB). The grace of God is not only for our salvation, but also for all that He provides for us in our day-to-day lives. God's grace can be manifested in the companions He graciously sends to us for our benefit *and* for our stewardship. To *not* receive a companion God sends or to not realize the potential in the relationship between our companions and ourselves would be to receive the grace of God in vain (1 Cor. 15:10; Gal. 2:21). Paul realized God's grace was being expressed to him in the companions God sent to Him. He was a good steward of this grace-gifting of God's.

THE SIN OF INDEPENDENCE

Paul learned how utterly foolish it was to try and function as an independent Christian. He knew very well that he never would have survived had he tried to "go it alone" in ministry. Companions, churches, apostles, emissaries, coworkers, yokefellows, fellow prisoners, and others were so utterly necessary that Paul treasured every one of them. As a car needs frequent refueling on a long journey, so his visits to the churches were times of spiritually refueling for him. He so desired to visit the church in Rome because, he said, "You and I may be *mutually encouraged* by each other's faith" (Rom 1:12 NIV, emphasis mine). He had much to offer them, but he very much needed their encouragement as well, as he said in Romans 15:32, "so that by God's will I may come to you with joy and *together with you* be refreshed" (NIV, emphasis mine). "After all," he wrote to the Thessalonians, "who is our hope, joy, or reason for boasting in the presence of our Lord Jesus at his coming? It is you, isn't it? Yes, you are our glory and joy!" (1 Thess. 2:19–20 ISV).

There are no better passages on interdependence in Paul's writings than in Romans 12 and 1 Corinthians 12 concerning the body of Christ. Paul not only applied this teaching on the body at the local church level, but to the kingdom of God, where churches need to work together for the common purpose of expanding God's kingdom. Churches, associations, conventions, denominations, ministries, foundations—wherever Christ is Lord—people need to work together.

To refuse to work with God's people is an affront to God. It is an embarrassment to Christ. It is a shameful act within the Christian community. To decline to cooperate with others to share the gospel, to minister to those in need, and to disciple, train, and equip the saints smacks of arrogance and selfish ambition (Phil. 2:3). "For everything that is in the world—the desire for fleshly gratification, the desire for possessions, and worldly arrogance—is not from the Father but is from the world" (1 John 2:16 ISV).

To refuse to work with God's people is an affront to God. It is an embarrassment to Christ.

How many pastors, ministry leaders, heads of Christian organizations, deacons, elders, committee chairpersons, and believers are still trying to accomplish God-given ministry tasks on their own, never realizing that assignments are given in *community*? God intends for the body of Christ to work together to accomplish what He asks them to do. To minister alone is to deny God's primary strategy in the New Testament. You might as well delete major chapters in Paul's letters to the churches if you are in a ministry that is isolated, independent, and uncooperative with other churches or organizations.

You may have been sent out alone by a mission organization, but that does not mean God expects you to be alone in ministry. Funding may have prohibited a companion from being sent with you, but look to see who God will bring alongside you in ministry. Some people, though, will not release their ministry into God's hands; they feel *they* must control it. So when God sends companions, they are seen as a threat instead of a blessing. How sad to reject the ones God sends, because it is ultimately God that is being rejected. Paul said, "Greet *every* saint in Christ Jesus" (Phil. 4:21, emphasis mine), not just those who are in your particular denomination, organization, or fraternity.

You may be amazed at what God is doing all around you through His people when you learn to accept the companions God sends you. Paul wrote to the Thessalonians, "But concerning brotherly love you have no need that I should write to you, for you yourselves are taught by God to love one another; and indeed you do so toward *all the brethren who are in all Macedonia*. But we urge you, brethren, that you increase more and more" (1 Thess. 4:9, emphasis mine).

God has always approached His people as a covenant community. Look back to the second book in the Bible:

> And you shall be to Me a kingdom of priests and a holy nation. These are the words which you shall speak to the children of Israel. So Moses came and called for the elders of the people, and laid before them all these words which the LORD commanded him. Then all the people answered together and said, "All that the LORD has spoken we will do." So Moses brought back the words of the people to the LORD. (Ex. 19:6–8)

Even when He worked with prophets, they were sent to the entire nation.

God does not play favorites among His people. They all can equally experience His grace, His gifts, His blessings, His joy, and His salvation as they give their hearts to Him. God's people are to be a kingdom of priests (see also 1 Peter 2:9–10), and we continue to serve Him as a royal priesthood, a chosen generation, a holy nation, and a special people that God has chosen out of darkness. God sees us both as individuals for whom Christ died *and* a people united in love, serving our Lord together with different faces, cultures, and nationalities.

Moses did not lead the children of Israel through the wilderness alone. Joshua did not defeat the city of Jericho alone. Peter did not spread the good news alone. And Paul never started a church alone. Each of these people worked in community to achieve what God wanted them to do. Jeremiah, the weeping prophet, was an example of a prophet with a ministry companion. He had a faithful scribe and colleague named Baruch (32:12–16; 36:4ff.; 45:1). Jeremiah's life as a prophet was intense, filled with opposition and persecution. But his faithful scribe walked with him through it all. Jeremiah spoke words from God, and Baruch wrote them down. What we enjoy reading today about Jeremiah's ministry is the result of Baruch's faithful companionship to him. For God's church and His people to accomplish His tasks in ministry, they must recapture the idea of interdependence, for it is at the core of all God does with His people.

THE SIN OF FOLLOWING THE WORLD'S MODELS INSTEAD OF GOD'S

You've probably read this Scripture many times, but reading it and applying it are two different things: "'For My thoughts are not your thoughts, nor are your ways My ways,' says the LORD. 'For as the heavens are higher than the earth, so are My ways higher than your ways, and My thoughts than your thoughts'" (Isa. 55:8–9). God did not confer with exit strategists when extricating His people from Egyptian slavery. He did not read up on military maneuverings when directing His people to defeat Jericho. He did not ask the advice of learned food-preparation specialists when feeding the five thousand. Neither did He seek man's wisdom when it came to redeeming a lost world.

Whether you are running an enormous Christian ministry or a two-staff church, if you want to know how God wants you to treat your companions, you should look to the Scriptures rather than the corporate world. I know of a church where the deacons didn't like the pastor. They wanted to fire him, so they looked to one of their businessmen in the congregation for advice on how a company lets go of an employee. Had they instead looked to David (1 Sam. 24:10) or even Elisha (2 Kings 2:23–24), they would have found that God's servants are not to be trifled with. Instead, this church treated God's servant with great disregard and no grace whatsoever, just as the world treats its employees. That church has paid a heavy price for how they have treated their pastors over the years.

On several occasions, Paul differentiates between the world (flesh, human nature) and the kingdom of God (spiritual nature, new man, "Christ in us"). They are set up as opposites and seen as incompatible with each other. Yet we want to use the world's methods and strategies for God's work as if the world knows how to accomplish God's goals. The truth is that the church needs to apply God's strategies to the corporate world, bringing truth, grace, love, compassion, and servant hearts to the workplace.

The companions (staff, coworkers, colleagues, etc.) God brings us are not simply staff to be hired and fired; they are God's servants, colaboring with us for a common purpose under a common Lord. The way we treat the ones God sends us is the way we are treating His Son. One of the main differences between a secular corporation and a church is that it is God who is working over all, in all, and through all of His people. We'd better check with the Master before we start treating any of His servants with any less compassion than He would treat them.

> **We'd better check with the Master before we start treating any of His servants with any less compassion than He would treat them.**

The Church never stops being the body of Christ because it has grown to more than a thousand in attendance. It doesn't suddenly become a corporation; it is still Christ's *body*, with Him at the head. He directs the members into positions of service and ministry and brings together those who can lead and guide the church to accomplish His will. He is still in charge, and the Scriptures are still validly applicable in every situation.

God's people love to invent *modern* ways to achieve God's purposes in ministry. But we sometimes forget that the New Testament is God's pattern for accomplishing His agenda. All the modern strategies, the contemporary models, and current methodologies put together pale in comparison to the global impact of what one small group of believers did two thousand years ago without any modern technology and resources. They had God and one another. Despite horrendous persecution and severe opposition, churches were planted, lives were transformed, and the message spread to the entire known world. Without the interdependence, the cooperation, the incessant prayers, and encouragement from one another, their mission—their mandate—would have met with quick disaster and defeat. We believe God is calling us to return to the fundamental New Testament model for ministry of Christian companionship.

A SERVANT OF GOD'S WITHOUT A COMPANION IS IN DANGER OF FALLING

There is no question that much of Paul's success in ministry was due to teamwork. Paul was not the only one who preached in the cities, discipled new believers, or baptized new converts; it was a *team effort*. His companions were indispensable to the work God gave Paul to do. Without the companions, colaborers, fellow prisoners, and groups of believers supporting him, Paul would never have left Antioch on his first missionary journey. Unfortunately, the truth of companionship is the missing component in many ministries today. A good number of people in ministry have no one working with them as a companion.

Elijah (1 Kings 17–21, 2 Kings 1–2) and Jonah are examples of God's prophets, loners for the most part, who could have used a companion. Both became frustrated, lonely, and fell into depressions, and in the end their ministries were compromised. King Saul (1 Sam. 9–31) was a leader without a companion. Though David was a faithful servant and soldier to Saul, Saul constantly rejected, threatened, and challenged him rather than allowing God to use David to help him.

I heard about a church member God chose to be a companion to a pastor. Unfortunately, it didn't dawn on the pastor what God was doing. The church member literally chased after the pastor on many occasions to be with him and to learn from him. This individual was relentless in his pursuit of discipleship, training, and equipping for ministry, because God's hand was on his life. God wants to do so much more than we can ever think or imagine in our ministries, and He will if we will only cooperate with what He wants to do through us.

APPRECIATE THE UNIQUE AND ETERNAL SIGNIFICANCE OF EVERY BELIEVER

Each believer has a special purpose and task to carry out in God's kingdom. But each is also designed as a body *part* (1 Cor. 12), that is, designed to fit perfectly in a greater whole. The uniqueness should be celebrated, as it is incredibly important to the body for it to function properly. The unique characteristics of each of Paul's companions helped to shape his life and ministry and to complement his weaknesses.

Though I enjoy singing and play a little piano (very little), most people would not consider me a musician or song leader. You can imagine my joy when God brought Ron and Pat Owens as companions. They have partnered with us for revival and awakening for more than fifteen years. God equipped them as musicians, and together they added a music and worship gift to our ministry that no one else had. They have faithfully given of their lives as God's blessing to us and have been an encouragement beyond measure over the years.

When Paul said, "Therefore I am pleased in weaknesses, in insults, in necessities, in persecutions, in distresses for Christ's sake; for when I am weak, then I am powerful" (2 Cor. 12:10 MKJV), he acknowledged Christ at work in his own life. But often, the strength of Christ comes in the form of a companion as He works through them to encourage us. Paul also said, "We then that are strong ought to bear the infirmities of the weak, and not to please ourselves. Let every one of us please his neighbour for his good, to edification [building up]" (Rom. 15:1–2 KJV).

I have often marveled at God's wonderful creativity when I see the variety of companions He has brought to me in ministry. I am so grateful that they were not all the same, nor were they just like me. Their originality, insight, and encouragement to pursue God's will often lifted me up at times when I was weary, lonely, and seeking a word from God for the way ahead. The command to "carry one another's burdens and so you will fulfill the law of Christ" (Gal. 6:2 MKJV) cannot be done alone. This is an integral part of companionship, one that was significant to Paul's ministry.

NEVER BE CASUAL ABOUT COMPANIONSHIP

The life of Paul gives evidence that companionship can literally mean life or death to some people. This is just as true in relationships, ministries, organizations, and evangelistic efforts.

Many marriages could be saved if there was a companion to walk with each couple. One young couple I know were going through the book *Preparing for Marriage* by Dennis Rainey. A mentoring couple, who had been married for more than ten years, reviewed each chapter with them. The older couple was open in sharing their own marriage experience, and the relationship proved invaluable to the new couple, as they later faced hard times in their own marriage.

Some young people might not try to take their lives if there were companions to walk with them. A young deacon in Tom's church confided that as a teenager he had intended to end his life. As he began to pull the gun's trigger, the doorbell rang. God had laid this young man on the heart of a youth worker and compelled him to go check on him at his home. That day a life was spared and a servant of God's discipled because of a companion God sent at just the right time.

Had George Mueller's letter not arrived encouraging Taylor to live by faith, Hudson Taylor may never have begun the China Inland Mission agency and accomplished all that God was able to do through him to reach thousands for Christ.

A companion can help keep a friend from falling into sin. Sin is more than moral failure or succumbing to degrading temptations. It can manifest itself as a critical spirit, a lack of faith in God, neglect of one's responsibilities, and even laziness. A good companion can identify when his friend is not functioning up to his potential and help him get back on the right track. The downward progression can be stopped and reversed through companionship.

My wife worked in an elderly-care home where many of the residents had no visitors, no companions, no one to care for them but the staff of the facility. No one came at Christmas, no one sent a card on their birthdays, and no one called to see how they were doing. She realized she had a marvelous opportunity to be an encourager to those who were alone in their last days. She sang hymns as she cleaned their rooms. She hummed gospel tunes as she washed down their bathrooms. She prayed for those who were lonely and dejected. It was not long before some of the residents began requesting her to sing their favorite hymns, ones they remembered from happier times in their lives. Her simple act of encouragement brought light back to dimming eyes.

A companion can help carry the load when it seems too much to bear. You may never know just how much your life can mean to others when you walk with them through life's challenges. The right word, the right act of kindness, the right tear shed at the right time can be all that is needed to lift up the weary, save the life of a brother or sister in Christ, and give new hope to the discouraged. Like the Good Samaritan, we do not have the right to walk on the other side of the road. Choosing to ignore those in need is to ignore Christ (Matt. 25:40).

> **Like the Good Samaritan, we do not have the right to walk on the other side of the road. Choosing to ignore those in need is to ignore Christ.**

Four or five people over the years have called to tell me that my book *Experiencing God* had meant a great deal to their pastors, who were dying of cancer. They wanted to know if I would be willing to call their pastors to bring a word of encouragement to them. How could I refuse such a request from these committed and dear friends? These pastors were utterly shocked when I called to speak a word of hope to them, because it was so unexpected. But they had friends who cared enough about them to do what it took to be a blessing to them. The few minutes I spent calling these dear brothers in Christ meant a great deal to them and have deeply blessed me in return (Heb. 12:1–13; Isa. 50:4–5).

Several places in the Old Testament talk about the *elders* at the gate (Josh. 20:4). There was a tradition where the elders would stand at the gates of the city and give counsel and judgment to those who needed it. Disputes were settled, fair business practices were ensured, and justice was served.

The older men and women of faith should be *watchmen of the gates* to the younger ones in the faith. They need to be counselors to young men and women who need the advice of the elder people around them. Older men and women should be friends and companions to younger men, women, and couples. The younger adults need the more mature adults for advisors and companions to help them through the difficult times in their lives, particularly when their parents are not believers. My parents both died before I was barely out of seminary, and I had no earthly father and mother to turn to for advice on marriage or raising a family. The church family became my advisors and counsel when I had no family member to turn to. In his later years, Paul, too, often gave counsel and advice to others.

We often have the privilege of passing on blessings given to us to mission pastors as an encouragement to them. Many times they have reported that it was that very gift that encouraged them to remain in their places of ministry at a very difficult time. Charles Spurgeon, the great English pastor and theologian, wrote a plethora of letters to encourage pastors and Christian workers. The timeliness of a gift, a letter of encouragement, a phone call, or an e-mail can make all the difference in the lives of our fellow workers.

MORE IS ACCOMPLISHED FASTER TOGETHER THAN IS ACCOMPLISHED ALONE

There is an unprecedented ability to impact the lives of God's servants and be encouragers today as never before. God has provided the Christian community today with more than enough wealth to fund all the work necessary to bring the gospel to the world. There is no reason for missionaries and workers to go hungry due to lack of financial support. Sunday school classes, church mission funds, designated offerings and gifts, fund-raisers, and many more avenues can not only provide salaries, but ministry budgets for mission efforts all over the world if we take seriously our role as companions to God's servants. Every indication reveals that God's people (especially the wealthy) have more financial resources available to release to God for His kingdom work now than at any time in history. God is holding us accountable as stewards of all He has entrusted into our hands.

There have never been more effective and incredibly fast ways to communicate with people around the globe than we have today. E-mail, mobile phones, satellite networks, and text messaging have almost made letter writing by hand obsolete. Rather than waiting a month for a letter to arrive, we send documents and receive replies in mere seconds from destinations on the other side of the planet. Prayer requests are disseminated instantly to thousands of people, and God's prayer warriors are called into action in support of a crisis in a remote part of the world. Teleconferencing, video links, and simultaneous broadcasting make support and training that was never before possible available to people.

Two of my children currently work in overseas ministries. They regularly receive notes of encouragement through electronic communication from people they have never met. For them to know that God's people are praying for them and taking the time to write notes of support lifts their spirits and encourages their hearts.

Most days I feel like my second home is an airplane because of how much I travel. Isn't it amazing that we can be watching world events as they occur on TV, in the comfort of our living rooms in the evening, and be standing there ourselves the next day?

> **Working against the odds in places of danger and want, companionship is not only wise, but also indispensable to ministry.**

My wife and I have traveled to more than ninety-six countries, and our fondest memories are with our missionaries. From studying the life of Paul and the practices of Christ, we deeply believe God's servants have a deep need for companions in ministry. Working against the odds in places of danger and want, companionship is not only wise, but also indispensable to ministry.

Many families go together to the mission fields to work alongside our missionaries. Our daughter and her husband have gone to Europe to plant churches. They say the greatest asset to them is families who come with their children. Their kids draw other kids to children's programs and other outreach activities. The young people who come to help lead sports clinics attract other teenagers. Many children and young people have come to Christ through these efforts, even from non-Christian backgrounds. Plan to go as a family on mission.

There are unprecedented numbers of volunteers that are willing and ready to go anywhere in the world. Their passports are valid, their vaccines are up-to-date, and their hearts are set to serve God wherever He sends them. Youth groups, adult choirs, work teams, professionals, ESL teachers—the list is endless—have given their lives into the hands of the Master to send them as encouragers and coworkers whenever and wherever He chooses. God matches the resources to the needs when we watch and listen for His activity. We are often surprised at where God's blessings came from, but we always know they came from Him.

There are entire networks of believers in churches, mission organizations, and Christian efforts all around the world to which God's people have access in times of need. Paul worked through the churches to help meet the needs of believers. When the brothers and sisters were starving in Jerusalem, he took up a collection from all the churches to help them. He was affirmed by the church in Jerusalem, sent out by the church in Antioch, cared for by the church in Philippi, and prayed for by all the churches as he helped to establish the interdependence of all the churches with one another.

Among the great resources God's people have are the vast prayer networks in place that can immediately put thousands of His people on their knees worldwide. This, perhaps, is the greatest moment in the larger context of companionship. People all over the world join together in prayer before the throne of God and lift up people and situations to His glory. What an inspiring and encouraging resource for God's people to access.

From the life of Paul, we see that God has purposed missionaries, especially in our day, to go with companions. If Paul's life is the model for missions, then no less than two individuals or couples should be sent to a mission field. When God commissioned Paul in Acts 13:2 ("Separate to Me Barnabas and Saul for the work to which I have called them"), He did so as a *pair*. Even Christ sent His disciples out in pairs (Mark 6:7) and later said, "Ask the Lord of the harvest, therefore, to send out workers [plural] into his harvest field" (Matt. 9:38 NIV). The harvest is great, but those working alone cannot accomplish what companions can achieve together.

Another interesting component to Paul's success was the collection of individuals who helped fund his ministry. Businesspeople like Lydia of Philippi sent money to support Paul during difficult times. Nicodemus and Joseph of Arimathea used their wealth and influence to minister to Christ and arranged to have His body cared for after the Crucifixion. Many persons in the first church sold possessions, land, and assets to assist those in need. This is a normal activity in God's economy: He blesses some people so they can be a blessing to others. There have been many people who have quietly underwritten mission and ministry projects over the years. They have been the silent partners, giving what they could so others could go and minister. The German prince, Elector Frederick of Saxony, became Martin Luther's (1483–1546) protector and benefactor, allowing him to complete the translation of the Bible into the common German language (1520s).

We don't know how much was raised in Philippi for Paul's needs, but we know that it was adequate, even more than enough (Phil. 4:14, 18). The church in Philippi became partners with Paul in his ministry through their gifts, encouragement, and through people they sent on their behalf (1:7).

FINISHING WELL

As we have seen, Paul was rarely found without a companion. During those times when he was alone, little to nothing was accomplished in terms of church planting (Athens, for example). So important were companions and friends to Paul that he nurtured relationships with others even across long distances. He went to great lengths to mention those important to him and even sent messengers to greet them on his behalf. In fact, the older Paul grew, the more dependent he became on others and the more needful others seemed to be to him. But Paul had developed companions over a lifetime so that when he was the neediest, there were many who could address his needs. Near the end of his ministry we find him making special requests to individuals (John Mark, Timothy, Silas) to join him as soon as possible. He also alluded to those who may have been watching over him throughout his ministry, as though cheering him on (Heb. 12:1).

If you could measure a man by the number of friends he possesses, Paul was a giant among men. I know the apostle John had Christ in mind when he wrote, "By this we know the love [of God], because He laid down His life for us. And we also ought to lay down our lives for the brethren" (1 John 3:16); and "Greater love has no one than this, than to lay down one's life for his friends" (John 15:13). But I can't help but imagine that he also had the example of Paul as one who most exemplified this verse. For one to inspire so many others to risk their lives for him, he must have demonstrated the same intentions toward them. To the Thessalonians Paul wrote, "We cared so much for you, and you became so dear to us, that we were willing to give our lives for you when we gave you God's message" (1 Thess. 2:8 CEV).

Many people begin their Christian lives well, but not as many finish well. Paul finished well. He could say with a clear conscience, "For I am already being poured out, and the time of my release is here. I have fought the good fight, I have finished the course, I have kept the faith. Now there is laid up for me the crown of righteousness, which the Lord, the righteous Judge, shall give me at that Day; and not to me only, but also to all those who love His appearing" (2 Tim. 4:6–8 MKJV). One of the greatest things a Christian can do as an encouragement to others is to finish well.

I know of many who have made poor choices at the end of their careers in ministry, and it is as though all they had worked for had been forgotten or wasted. Ending a ministry in disgrace, in sin, in moral failure will be the last thing people remember about many who started well. Paul was always cognizant of the multitudes watching his life and did not want to do anything that would be a stumbling block to them. He was faithful right to the end and was ready to receive the "crown of righteousness" as a reward.

Paul offered this word of advice to believers, because he knew how important building strong friendships would be to them in the days of persecution that were just ahead: "Keep on loving each other as brothers. Do not forget to entertain strangers, for by so doing some people have entertained angels without knowing it. Remember those in prison as if you were their fellow prisoners, and those who are mistreated as if you yourselves were suffering" (Heb. 13:1–3 NIV).

There were several people to whom I could have been a better companion over the years. Somehow it was far too easy to become so focused on the ministry at hand than on those people God called to labor beside me. I have realized that the ministry and the journey are only half the fun. Seeing God working through you and your companions is the other half.

There is a great line spoken by an anonymous young man who bore the armor of Prince Jonathan when the prince suggested they go up together and fight a Philistine outpost: "Do all that is in your heart. Go . . . I am with you, according to your heart" (1 Sam. 14:7). What a great picture of companionship! "I am with you, according to your heart" is the theme of every companion God sends to you: kindred spirits, hearts knitted together, with a shared objective and a common Lord.

Let me end with this exhortation from Paul himself to the Philippian believers. As you read it, see it in the light of companionship:

> You know the teachings I gave you, and you know what you heard me say and saw me do. So follow my example. And God, who gives peace, will be with you. (Phil. 4:9 CEV)

STUDY QUESTIONS

1. In what ways has your concept of companionship been expanded in this chapter?

2. Can you see ways in which God may be calling you to a type of companionship that will use the gifts He has given you?

3. Are there people you know right now who you sense need a companion in their lives? What do you think you could do about it?

4. Are there people in your life like Paul who left you an encouraging example by *finishing well*?

5. Can you see how damaging independence can be to a person's ministry and to the kingdom of God?

6. For what areas of weakness do you think God may want to bring companions to help you?

7. Can you identify people whom God sent to you as companions but you rejected? Though the opportunity may be lost, there is still time to build a relationship that God may still want to use in your ministry.

8. Which role do you think is more demanding: to *be* a companion to one of God's leaders, or to *have* God-sent companions (whom you are to treat as you would treat Christ)?

9. God saw that it was not good for Adam to be alone (Gen. 2:18). Take a moment to write down a list of the benefits of companionship. Then pray, asking God to help you be a godly companion to others and to bring godly companions to you, that your ministry may multiply in its effectiveness.

Appendix A

Names of Paul's Friends by Book and Chapter

Acts

9	Ananias, Barnabas
13	Simeon, Lucius, Manaen, John Mark
15	Judas, Silas
16	Timothy, Lydia, Philippian jailer
17	Jason, Dionysius, Damaris
18	Sosthenes, Aquila, Priscilla, Apollos
19	Erastus
20	Sopater, Aristarchus, Secundus, Gaius, Tychicus, Trophimus
21	Philip the Evangelist, Agabus

Romans

16   Aquila, Priscilla, Phoebe, Epenetus, Mary, Andronicus, Junias, Ampliatus, Urbanus, Stachys, Apelles, Aristobulus, Herodion, Narcissus, Tryphena, Tryphosa, Persis, Rufus (and his mother), Asyncritus, Phlegon, Hermas, Patrobas, Hermas, Philologus, Julia, Nereus, Olympas, Sosipater, Tertius, Gaius, Erastus

1 CORINTHIANS

1	Sosthenes, Apollos, Gaius, Cephas, Crispus, Chloe, Stephanas
16	Achaicus, Aquila, Priscilla, Fortunatus

2 CORINTHIANS

1	Timothy
2	Titus
7	Titus
8	Titus
12	Titus

GALATIANS

1	Peter, James
2	Barnabas, Titus, John

EPHESIANS

6	Tychicus

PHILIPPIANS

1	Timothy
2	Epaphroditus
4	Euodia, Syntyche, Clement, Epaphroditus

COLOSSIANS

1	Timothy
4	Archippus, Tychicus, Onesimus, Justus, Aristarchus, Mark, Epaphras, Luke, Demas, Nympha

1 THESSALONIANS

1	Silas, Timothy

2 THESSALONIANS

1   Silas, Timothy

1 TIMOTHY

1   Timothy

2 TIMOTHY

1   Timothy, Lois, Eunice, Phygelus, Hermogenes, Onesiphorus

4   Aquila, Carpus, Claudia, Crescens, Erastus, Eubulus, Linus, Luke, Mark, Onesiphorus, Priscilla, Pudens, Titus, Tychicus

TITUS

1   Titus

3   Artemas, Tychicus, Zenas, Apollos

PHILEMON

1   Philemon, Apphia, Archippus, Epaphras, Mark, Aristarchus, Demas, Luke, Timothy, Onesimus

PAUL'S JOURNEYS

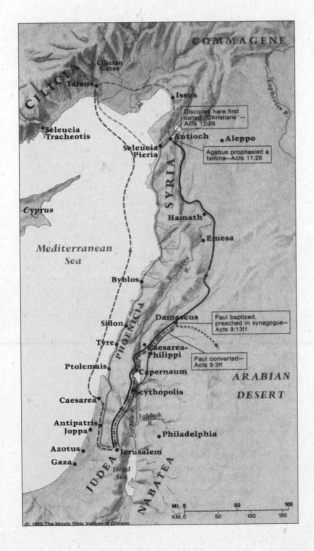

- ● city
- ⋈ mountain pass
- ——— Paul (Saul) commissioned to journey to Damascus and seek out Christians (Acts 9:1)
- ----- Paul Spent time in Arabia (Gal. 1:17)
- ‒·‒· Paul returned to Jerusalem and was received by disciples (Acts 9:26f)
- ‒ ‒ ‒ Paul Fled from Hellenists (Acts 9:28f)
- ‒ ‒ ‒ Barnabas journeyed to Tarsus and returned to Antioch with Paul (Acts 11:25f)
- ——— Paul & Barnabas sent to Jerusalem with aid for believers amidst famine (Acts 11:29f)
- ━━━ Paul & Barnabas returned to Antioch, joined by John Mark (Acts 12:25)

MAP ONE: PAUL'S EARLY TRAVELS

COMMAGENE

CILICIA

Cilician Gates

Tarsus

Issus

Euphrates R.

Disciples here first called "Christians"— Acts 11:26

Seleucia Tracheotis

Aleppo

Antioch

Seleucia Pieria

SYRIA

Agabus prophesied a famine—Acts 11:28

Cyprus

Hamath

Mediterranean Sea

Emesa

Orontes R.

Byblos

Damascus

Paul baptized, preached in synagogue— Acts 9:13ff

Sidon

PHOENICIA

Tyre

Caesarea-Philippi

Paul converted— Acts 9:3ff

Ptolemais

Capernaum

ARABIAN DESERT

Scythopolis

Caesarea

Antipatris

Jabbok R.

Joppa

Jordan R.

Philadelphia

Azotus

Jerusalem

Gaza

JUDEA

Dead Sea

NABATEA

MI. 0   50   100

KM. 0   50   100   150

© 1985 The Moody Bible Institute of Chicago

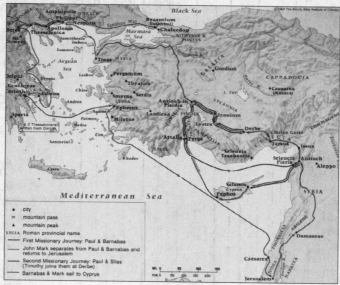

MAP TWO:
PAUL'S FIRST AND SECOND JOURNEYS

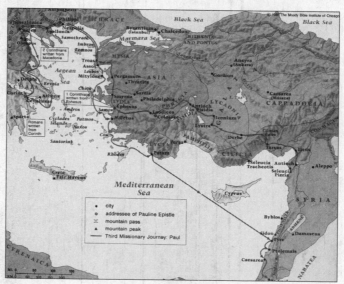

MAP THREE:
PAUL'S THIRD JOURNEY

MAP FOUR:

PAUL'S TRIP TO ROME

List of Companions by City of Origin or First Acquaintance with Paul

Ananias	– Damascus
Apollos	– Alexandria
Aristarchus	– Thessalonica
Barnabas	– Cyprus
Epaphras	– Colosse
Epaphroditus	– Philippi
John Mark	– Jerusalem
Luke	– Antioch
Lydia	– Philippi (Thyatira)
Onesimus	– Colosse
Onesiphorus	– Ephesus
Peter	– Jerusalem (Galilee)
Philemon	– Colosse
Phoebe	– Cenchrea
Priscilla and Aquila	– Corinth (Rome)
Silvanus (or Silas)	– Jerusalem
Timothy	– Lystra
Titus	– Antioch (?)
Tychicus	– Asia (?)

LYSTRA

Lystra is a town located in the eastern part of the great plain of Lycaonia in Asia Minor. It was eighteen miles South-Southwest from Iconium. The inhabitants were from the aristocracy of Roman soldiers who formed the local garrison, as well as Greeks, Jews, and native Lycaonians. Lystra was made a Roman *colonia* by Augustus, and during Paul's day was a center of education and enlightenment. Timothy, his mother, and grandmother were residents here. Today, the site of Lystra may be identified with the ruins of *Bin-bir-Kilisseh*.

ANTIOCH

Antioch (named by Seleucus Nicator after his father Antiochus in 301 BC) is located in Syria and was the capital of the Greek kings of Syria, and later served as the residence of Roman governors. It lies at a bend of the Orontes River, 16½ miles from the Mediterranean, 300 miles north of Jerusalem. Antioch, in Paul's time, contained over two hundred thousand inhabitants and thrived under the Seleucid kings becoming a place of great beauty with important structures such as aqueducts, amphitheatres, and baths. It was called the "first city of the East" and ranked third, after Rome and Alexandria, in importance of all the cities in the Roman Empire.

Jerusalem alone played a more important role in the establishment of churches next to Antioch. It was in Antioch were the first Gentile church was founded and where followers of Christ were first called Christians. Antioch was the cradle of Gentile Christianity and of the Christian missionary enterprise. It was the church at Antioch who persuaded the council at Jerusalem to relieve Gentile Christians of the burden of the Jewish law (Acts 15). Antioch was Paul's starting point in his three missionary journeys, and where he returned to after his first two journeys. The most notable Christian to come from Antioch was John Chrysostom. Antioch still bears its ancient name, *Antakiyeh*.

CORINTH

Corinth was an ancient and celebrated city of Greece, on the Isthmus of Corinth. It lies about forty miles west of Athens forming the most direct communication between the Ionian and Aegean seas. Corinth had three good harbors (Lechaeum, on the Corinthian, and Cenchrea and Schoenus on the Saronic Gulf) and governed the traffic of the eastern and the western seas. It became the seat of government for southern Greece or Achaia (Acts 18:12–16). It was noted for its wealth and for the luxurious, immoral, and vicious habits of the people. It had a large mixed population of Romans, Greeks, and Jews.

The Corinthian cult of Aphrodite, of Melikertes (Melkart) and of Athene Phoenike, as well as Poseidon and other sea deities, was held in high esteem in this commercial city. Various arts were developed as the Corinthians were noted for their cleverness, inventiveness, and artistic sense. They took much pride in surpassing the other Greeks in the embellishment of their city and in the adornment of their temples.

When Paul first visited the city (AD 51 or 52), he stayed for eighteen months (Acts 18:1–18) after becoming acquainted with Aquila and Priscilla. After an interval he visited it a second time and remained for three months (Acts 20:3), writing his epistle to the Romans (probably AD 55). Although there were many Jewish converts at Corinth, the Gentiles were in the clear majority in the church there. Paul had intended to make the city of Thessalonica his base of operations, but his plans were changed by a revelation. In it the Lord commanded him to speak boldly, and he did so, establishing one of the stronger churches in Asia Minor. Two of his letters were written to the church in Corinth.

EPHESUS

Ephesus was a city of the Roman province of Asia, near the mouth of the Cayster river, three miles from the western coast of Asia Minor, and opposite the island of Samos. Its artificial harbor was accessible to the largest ships rivaling the harbor at Miletus. In the time of the Romans, Ephesus bore the title "the first and greatest metropolis of Asia." It was known for its theatre, which was the largest in the world, capable of holding fifty thousand spectators. However its wealth and prominence are largely due to the great Temple of Diana.

Ephesus was the most easily accessible city in Asia, both by land and sea, and was well-developed in religion, politics, and commercial enterprise. Ephesus provided Paul with an excellent location for sharing the gospel. It was to this city that Paul returned at the close of his second missionary journey (about AD 51) and left Aquila and Priscilla behind him to continue developing the new church. During his third missionary journey, Paul reached Ephesus from the upper coasts and remained there for about three years, having noticeable fruit from his labours. On his return from his journey, Paul stopped briefly at Miletus, some thirty miles south of Ephesus, where he met with Ephesian church leaders.

Ephesus was dear to Paul's heart and received at least two of his companions (Timothy and Tychicus) to encourage them. Two of Paul's companions, Trophimus and Tychicus, were probably natives of Ephesus. In his second epistle to Timothy, Paul spoke of Onesiphorus as having served him in many ways at Ephesus. Ephesus is twice mentioned in the book of Revelation and, according to tradition, the apostle John spent many years in Ephesus, where he died and was buried.

PHILIPPI

Philippi was the capital of the province of Macedonia, named for Philip of Macedonia. It stood near the head of the Sea, about eight miles north-west of the island of Thasos, which is twelve miles from Neapolis, the modern *Kavalla*. Philippi is on the Egnatian Road, thirty-three Roman miles from Amphipolis and twenty-one from Acontisma. The Philippi known by Paul was a Roman colony founded by Augustus after the famous battle of Philippi, fought there between Antony and Octavius and Brutus and Cassius, 42 BC.

Philippi was the first city in Europe to hear the gospel, and Lydia was its first convert. Here, Paul and Silas were imprisoned and met with their miraculous escape, leading to the conversion of the jailor and his house-hold. Later the Philippians sent contributions to Paul to relieve his needs. Some believe Dr. Luke was from this city because of the change from the third to the first person in Acts 16:10, perhaps marking the point at which Luke joined Paul's missionary band. Luke remained at Philippi between Paul's first and his third visit to the city.

ROME

Rome was the most celebrated city in the world at the time of Christ and was said to have been founded in 753 BC. Rome, known for its wealth and luxury, was enriched and adorned with the spoils of the world, which it largely controlled. During New Testament times, Rome's influence could be seen in every city and on every major road in the empire. Roman citizens were divided into three classes: senatorial, equestrian, and plebeian with a tiny upper class, no middle class, and no free industrial population. Of the estimated population of 1,200,000, half were slaves representing

185

nearly every known nation. Beneath this city are extensive galleries, called *catacombs*, which were used from about the time of the apostles (circa AD 71) for some three hundred years as places of refuge in the time of persecution, and also of worship and burial, giving an interesting insight into the history of the church down to the time of Constantine.

Romans were present in Jerusalem on the day of Pentecost and likely brought back news to Rome of God's workings with them. It may have been these Romans who were instrumental in beginning the church to whom Paul would later write his letter. Paul was brought to this city a prisoner, where he remained for two years and wrote his epistles to the Philippians, to the Ephesians, to the Colossians, to Philemon, and probably also to the Hebrews. Luke, Aristarchus, Timothy, Tychicus, Epaphroditus, and John Mark all spent time with Paul during his stay in Rome.

THESSALONICA

The original name of this city was *Therma*. Cassander, the son of Antipater, rebuilt and enlarged Therma, and named it after his wife, Thessalonica, the sister of Alexander the Great. It became the most populous city in Macedonia and was the chief station on the Roman road *Via Egnatia*, connecting Rome to the regions north of the Aegean.

Thessalonica was an invaluable center for the spread of the gospel. In fact, it rivaled Corinth and Ephesus in commerce and trade. Paul visited Thessalonica (with Silas and Timothy) during his second missionary journey, and introduced Christianity there. It is recorded that he continued there for three weeks (Acts 17:2) and that a flourishing church was formed there. This city was to play an important role in Christianity for centuries to come. It is known today as *Saloniki*.

COLOSSE

Colosse was a city of Phrygia in Asia Minor, in the upper part of the basin of the Maeander, on the Lycus. Hierapolis and Laodicea were in its immediate neighborhood. Paul is likely to have visited Colosse and founded or confirmed the Colossian church on his third missionary journey.

TARSUS

Founded by Sardanapalus, king of Assyria, Tarsus became the chief town of Cilicia. It stood on the banks of the river Cydnus, about twelve miles north of the Mediterranean. In the civil wars of Rome, it took Caesar's aide, and on the occasion of a visit from him, had its name changed to Juliopolis. Augustus made it a "free city." It was renowned as a place of education under the early Roman emperors, being distinguished for its wealth and for its schools of learning, in which it rivaled even Athens and Alexandria. Cleopatra, when she visited Antony at his residence in Tarsus in 38 BC, was able to sail her richly decorated barge into the very heart of the city. Tarsus also was a place of much commerce. It is the birthplace and early residence of the apostle Paul, which allowed him the privileges of Roman citizenship.

SOURCES

Easton's Bible Dictionary, M. G. Easton M.A., D.D., 1897.

New Bible Dictionary (NBD), J. D. Douglas, organizing editor, InterVarsity Press, Leicester, England, 1962.

International Standard Bible Encyclopedia, James Orr, M.A., D.D., general editor, Hendrickson Publishers, 1994.

Smith's Bible Dictionary, Dr. William Smith, 1884.

Journey's of Paul: from Tarsus 'to the ends of the earth' (JOP), Fatih Cimok, A Turizm Yayinlari (Istanbul, Turkey, 2004)

(TCSB) *Thompson Chain-Reference Bible* NIV Archeological Supplement, G. Grederick Owen, Zondervan Bible Publishers, Grand Rapids Michigan, 1983.

ABOUT THE AUTHORS

HENRY BLACKABY and his wife Marilynn have five children, all of whom are actively serving in full-time Christian ministry. They also have fourteen grandchildren. Dr. Blackaby graduated from the University of British Columbia and Golden Gate Baptist Theological Seminary. He has also been granted four honorary doctoral degrees. He has authored numerous books, many with his children. His best-known work is *Experiencing God: Knowing and Doing the Will of God*. He is the author of the Biblical Legacy Series, and previously coauthored eight books with his son Richard, including *Experiencing God: Day by Day; Spiritual Leadership: Moving People on to God's Agenda;* and *Hearing God's Voice*. Dr. Blackaby speaks worldwide and regularly consults with Christian CEOs in America on issues related to spiritual leadership.

TOM BLACKABY has served in churches in three different countries for more than twenty years in the areas of worship, youth ministry, administration, and Christian education. He and his father have previously coauthored *The Man God Uses*, and he has been a devotional writer for Christian magazines for four years. Tom has earned a bachelor of education, a master of theology, and a doctor of ministry. He now serves as senior pastor of North Sea Baptist Church in Stavanger Norway, where he lives with his wife, Kim, and their three children, Erin, Matthew, and Conor.

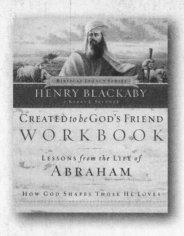
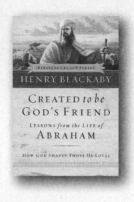

From the example of the life of Abraham, Henry Blackaby will show you how to become God's intimate friend. In this the first book in the Biblical Legacy Series, you will learn how God shapes those He loves into useful, joyful co-workers as they hear and respond to His call in everyday life. *Created to Be God's Friend* is a remarkable study of our relationship with a personal God who is constantly working in each of our lives.

Book ISBN: 0-7852-6982-7
Workbook ISBN: 0-7852-6758-1

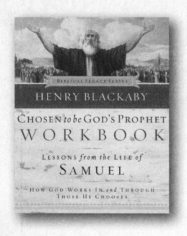
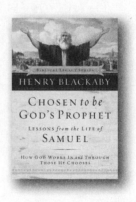

Samuel's life was full of incredible—and defining—moments as God shaped him and guided him. As readers observe how God moved in Samuel's life, they will recognize those moments in their own lives; moments that are so different from the run-of-the-mill ones. God uses these "divine moments," which often come during times of crisis, to bring His purposes to pass. By taking a glimpse into what God did in Samuel's life, Dr. Blackaby enables readers to define those critical times in their lives when God selects us as His chosen servants. *Chosen to Be God's Prophet* is the second selection in the Biblical Legacy Series offered by Thomas Nelson Publishers.

Book ISBN: 0-7852-6555-4
Workbook ISBN: 0-7852-6557-0

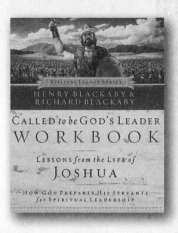
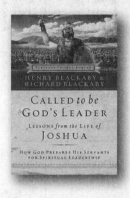

What did God have in mind when He saw Joshua as a young slave in Egypt? How did He mold and shape Joshua to prepare him for service? Through Joshua and numerous examples from their own lives, the authors create a picture of God's ways, offering deep insight that readers can apply to their own lives. Purpose, Obedience, Faith, Character, and Influence are among the themes that are included in the book; key truths are emphasized at the end of each chapter.

Book ISBN: 0-7852-6203-2
Workbook ISBN: 0-7852-6204-0